Socialism and Mod

CW00516785

(Darwin, Spencer, Marx)

Enrico Ferri

Alpha Editions

This edition published in 2023

ISBN : 9789357969505

Design and Setting By
Alpha Editions
www.alphaedis.com
Email - info@alphaedis.com

Contents

Author's Preface.

(For the French Edition.)

This volume—which it has been desired to make known to the great public in the French language—in entering upon a question so complex and so vast as socialism, has but a single and definite aim.

My intention has been to point out, and in nearly all cases by rapid and concise observations, the general relations existing between contemporary socialism and the whole trend of modern scientific thought.

The opponents of contemporary socialism see in it, or wish to see in it, merely a reproduction of the sentimental socialism of the first half of the Nineteenth Century. They contend that socialism is in conflict with the fundamental facts and inductions of the physical, biological and social sciences, whose marvelous development and fruitful applications are the glory of our dying century.

To oppose socialism, recourse has been had to the individual interpretations and exaggerations of such or such a partisan of Darwinism, or to the opinions of such or such a sociologist—opinions and interpretations in obvious conflict with the premises of their theories on universal and inevitable evolution.

It has also been said—under the pressure of acute or chronic hunger—that "if science was against socialism, so much the worse for science." And those who thus spoke were right if they meant by "science"—even with a capital S—the whole mass of observations and conclusions *ad usum delphini* that orthodox science, academic and official—often in good faith, but sometimes also through interested motives—has always placed at the disposal of the ruling minorities.

I have believed it possible to show that modern experiential science is in complete harmony with contemporary socialism, which, since the work of Marx and Engels and their successors, differs essentially from sentimental socialism, both in its scientific system and in its political tactics, though it continues to put forth generous efforts for the attainment of the same goal: social justice for all men.

I have loyally and candidly maintained my thesis on scientific grounds; I have always recognized the partial truths of the theories of our opponents, and I have not ignored the glorious achievements of the bourgeoisie and bourgeois science since the outbreak of the French Revolution. The disappearance of the bourgeois class and science, which, at their advent marked the disappearance of the hieratic and aristocratic classes and science, will result in the triumph of social justice for all mankind, without distinction of classes, and in the triumph of truth carried to its ultimate consequences.

The appendix contains my replies to a letter of Herbert Spencer and to an anti-socialist book of M. Garofalo. It shows the present state of social science, and of the struggle between ultra-conservative orthodoxy, which is blinded to the sad truths of contemporary life by its traditional syllogisms and innovating heterodoxy which is ever becoming more marked among the learned, as well as strengthening its hold upon the collective intelligence.

ENRICO FERRI.

Brussels, Nov., 1895.

Introduction.

Convinced Darwinian and Spencerian, as I am, it is my intention to demonstrate that Marxian Socialism—the only socialism which has a truly scientific method and value, and therefore the only socialism which from this time forth has power to inspire and unite the Social Democrats throughout the civilized world—is only the practical and fruitful fulfilment, in the social life, of that modern scientific revolution which—inaugurated some centuries since by the rebirth of the experimental method in all branches of human knowledge—has triumphed in our times, thanks to the works of Charles Darwin and Herbert Spencer.

It is true that Darwin and especially Spencer halted when they had travelled only half way toward the conclusions of a religious, political or social order, which necessarily flow from their indisputable premises. But that is, as it were, only an individual episode, and has no power to stop the destined march of science and of its practical consequences, which are in wonderful accord with the necessities—necessities enforced upon our attention by want and misery—of contemporary life. This is simply one more reason why it is incumbent upon us to render justice to the scientific and political work of Karl Marx which completes the renovation of modern scientific thought.

Feeling and thought are the two inseparable impelling forces of the individual life and of the collective life.

Socialism, which was still, but a few years since, at the mercy of the strong and constantly recurring but undisciplined fluctuations of humanitarian sentimentalism, has found, in the work of that great man, Karl Marx, and of those who have developed and completed his thought, its scientific and political guide.[1] This is the explanation of every one of its conquests.

Civilization is the most fruitful and most beautiful development of human energies, but it contains also an infectious *virus* of tremendous power. Beside the splendor of its artistic, scientific and industrial achievements, it accumulates gangrenous products, idleness, poverty, misery, insanity, crime and physical suicide and moral suicide, *i. e.* servility.

Pessimism—that sad symptom of a life without ideals and, in part, the effect of the exhaustion or even of the degeneration of the nervous system—glorifies the final annihilation of all life and sensation as the only mode of escaping from or triumphing over pain and suffering.

We have faith, on the contrary, in the eternal *virtus medicatrix naturae* (healing power of Nature), and socialism is precisely that breath of a new and better life which will free humanity—after some access of fever perhaps—from the noxious products of the present phase of civilization, and which, in a more advanced phase, will give a new power and opportunity of expansion to all the healthy and fruitful energies of all human beings.

ENRICO FERRI.

Rome, June, 1894.

FOOTNOTE:

[1] The word in the original means a mariner's compass.—*Tr.*

PART FIRST.

I.

VIRCHOW AND HAECKEL AT THE CONGRESS OF MUNICH.

On the 18th of September, 1877, Ernest Haeckel, the celebrated embryologist of Jena, delivered at the Congress of Naturalists, which was held at Munich, an eloquent address defending and propagating Darwinism, which was at that time the object of the most bitter polemical attacks.

A few days afterward, Virchow, the great pathologist,—an active member of the "progressive" parliamentary party, hating new theories in politics just as much as in science—violently assailed the Darwinian theory of organic evolution, and, moved by a very just presentiment, hurled against it this cry of alarm, this political anathema: "Darwinism leads directly to socialism."

The German Darwinians, and at their head Messrs. Oscar Schmidt and Haeckel, immediately protested; and, in order to avert the addition of strong political opposition to the religious, philosophical, and biological opposition already made to Darwinism, they maintained, on the contrary, that the Darwinian theory is in direct, open and absolute opposition to socialism.

"If the Socialists were prudent," wrote Oscar Schmidt in the "Ausland" of November 27, 1877, "they would do their utmost to kill, by silent neglect, the theory of descent, for that theory most emphatically proclaims that the socialist ideas are impracticable."

"As a matter of fact," said Haeckel,[2] "there is no scientific doctrine which proclaims more openly than the theory of descent that the equality of individuals, toward which socialism tends, is an impossibility; that this chimerical equality is in absolute contradiction with the necessary and, in fact, universal inequality of individuals.

"Socialism demands for all citizens equal rights, equal duties, equal possessions and equal enjoyments; the theory of descent establishes, on the contrary, that the realization of these hopes is purely and simply impossible; that, in human societies, as in animal societies, neither the rights, nor the duties, nor the possessions, nor the enjoyments of all the members of a society are or ever can be equal.

"The great law of variation teaches—both in the general theory of evolution and in the smaller field of biology where it becomes the theory of descent—that the variety of phenomena flows from an original unity, the diversity of functions from a primitive identity, and the complexity of organization from a primordial simplicity. The conditions of existence for all individuals are, from their very birth, unequal. There must also be taken into consideration the inherited qualities and the innate tendencies which also vary more or less widely. In view of all this, how can the work and the reward be equal for all?

"The more highly the social life is developed, the more important becomes the great principle of the division of labor, the more requisite it becomes for the stable existence of the State as a whole that its members should distribute among themselves the multifarious tasks of life, each performing a single function; and as the labor which must be performed by the individuals, as well as the expenditure of strength, talent, money, etc., which it necessitates, differs more and more, it is natural that the remuneration of this labor should also vary widely. These are facts so simple and so obvious that it seems to me every intelligent and enlightened statesman ought to be an advocate of the theory of descent and the general doctrine of evolution, as the best antidote for the absurd equalitarian, utopian notions of the socialists.

"And it was Darwinism, the theory of selection, that Virchow, in his denunciation, had in mind, rather than mere metamorphic development, the theory of descent, with which it is always confused! Darwinism is anything rather than socialistic.

"If one wishes to attribute a political tendency to this English theory,— which is quite permissible,—this tendency can be nothing but aristocratic; by no means can it be democratic, still less socialistic.

"The theory of selection teaches that in the life of mankind, as in that of plants and animals, it is always and everywhere a small privileged minority alone which succeeds in living and developing itself; the immense majority, on the contrary, suffer and succumb more or less prematurely. Countless are the seeds and eggs of every species of plants and animals, and the young individuals who issue from them. But the number of those who have the good fortune to reach fully developed maturity and to attain the goal of their existence is relatively insignificant.

"The cruel and pitiless 'struggle for existence' which rages everywhere throughout animated nature, and which in the nature of things must rage, this eternal and inexorable competition between all living beings, is an undeniable fact. Only a small picked number of the strongest or fittest is able to come forth victoriously from this battle of competition. The great majority of their unfortunate competitors are inevitably destined to perish. It is well enough to deplore this tragic fatality, but one cannot deny it or change it. 'Many are called, but few are chosen!'

"The selection, the 'election' of these 'elect' is by absolute necessity bound up with the rejection or destruction of the vast multitude of beings whom they have survived. And so another learned Englishman has called the fundamental principle of Darwinism 'the survival of the fittest, the victory of the best.'

"At all events, the principle of selection is not in the slightest degree democratic; it is, on the contrary, thoroughly aristocratic. If, then, Darwinism, carried out to its ultimate logical consequences, has, according to Virchow, for the statesman 'an extraordinarily dangerous side,' the danger is doubtless that it favors aristocratic aspirations."

I have reproduced complete and in their exact form all the arguments of Haeckel, because they are those which are repeated—in varying tones, and with expressions which differ from his only to lose precision and eloquence—by those opponents of socialism who love to appear scientific, and who, for polemical convenience, make use of those ready-made or stereotyped phrases which have currency, even in science, more than is commonly imagined.

It is easy, nevertheless, to demonstrate that, in this debate, Virchow's way of looking at the subject was the more correct and more perspicacious, and that the history of these last twenty years has amply justified his position.

It has happened, indeed, that Darwinism and socialism have both progressed with a marvelous power of expansion. From that time the one was to conquer—for its fundamental theory—the unanimous endorsement of naturalists; the other was to continue to develop—in its general aspirations as in its political discipline—flooding all the conduits of the social consciousness, like a torrential inundation from internal wounds caused by the daily growth of physical and moral disease, or like a gradual, capillary, inevitable infiltration into minds freed from all prejudices, and which are not satisfied by the merely personal advantages that they derive from the orthodox distribution of spoils.

But, as political or scientific theories are natural phenomena and not the capricious and ephemeral products of the free wills of those who construct and propagate them, it is evident that if these two currents of modern thought have each been able to triumph over the opposition they first aroused—the strongest kind of opposition, scientific and political conservatism—and if every day increases the army of their avowed disciples, this of itself is enough to show us—I was about to say by a law of intellectual *symbiosis*—that they are neither irreconcilable with, nor contradictory to, each other.

Moreover, the three principal arguments which form the substance of the anti-socialist reasoning of Haeckel resist neither the most elementary criticisms, nor the most superficial observation of every-day life.

These arguments are:

I.—Socialism tends toward a chimerical equality of persons and property: Darwinism, on the contrary, not only establishes, but shows the organic necessity of the natural inequality of the capabilities and even the wants of individuals.

II.—In the life of mankind, as in that of plants and animals, the immense majority of those who are born are destined to perish, because only a small minority can triumph in the "struggle for existence"; socialism asserts, on the contrary, that all ought to triumph in this struggle, and that no one is inexorably destined to be conquered.

III.—The struggle for existence assures "the survival of the best, the victory of the fittest," and this results in an aristocratic hierarchic gradation of selected individuals—a continuous progress—instead of the democratic, collectivist leveling of socialism.

FOOTNOTE:

[2] Les preuves du transformisme.—Paris, 1879, page 110 *et seq.*

II.

THE EQUALITY OF INDIVIDUALS.

The first of the objections, which is brought against socialism in the name of Darwinism, is absolutely without foundation.

If it were true that socialism aspires to "the equality of all individuals," it would be correct to assert that Darwinism irrevocably condemns it.[3]

But although even to-day it is still currently repeated—by some in good faith, like parrots who recite their stereotyped phrases; by others in bad faith, with polemical skillfulness—that socialism is synonymous with equality and leveling; the truth is, on the contrary, that scientific socialism—the socialism which draws its inspiration from the theory of Marx, and which alone to-day is worthy of support or opposition,—has never denied the inequality of individuals, as of all living beings—inequality innate and acquired, physical and intellectual.[4]

It is just as if one should say that socialism asserts that a royal decree or a popular vote could settle it that "henceforth all men shall be five feet seven inches tall."

But in truth, socialism is something more serious and more difficult to refute.

Socialism says: *Men are unequal, but they are all* (of them) *men*.

And, in fact, although each individual is born and develops in a fashion more or less different from that of all other individuals,—just as there are not in a forest two leaves identically alike, so in the whole world there are not two men in all respects equals, the one of the other,—nevertheless every man, simply because he is a *human being*, has a right to the existence of a man, and not of a slave or a beast of burden.

We know, we as well as our opponents, that all men cannot perform the same kind and amount of labor—now, when social inequalities are added to equalities of natural origin—and that they will still be unable to do it under a socialist regime—when the social organization will tend to reduce the effect of congenital inequalities.

There will always be some people whose brains or muscular systems will be better adapted for scientific work or for artistic work, while others will be more fit for manual labor, or for work requiring mechanical precision, etc.

What ought not to be, and what will not be—is that there should be some men who do not work at all, and others who work too much or receive too little reward for their toil.

But we have reached the height of injustice and absurdity, and in these days it is the man who does not work who reaps the largest returns, who is thus guaranteed the individual monopoly of wealth which accumulates by means of hereditary transmission. This wealth, moreover, is only very rarely due to the economy and abstinence of the present possessor or of some industrious ancestor of his; it is most frequently the time-honored fruit of spoliation by military conquest, by unscrupulous "business" methods, or by the favoritism of sovereigns; but it is in every instance always independent of any exertion, of any socially useful labor of the inheritor, who often squanders his property in idleness or in the whirlpool of a life as inane as it is brilliant in appearance.

And, when we are not confronted with a fortune due to inheritance, we meet with wealth due to fraud. Without talking for the moment of the economic organization, the mechanism of which Karl Marx has revealed to us, and which, even without fraud, normally enables the capitalist or property owner to live upon his income without working, it is indisputable that the fortunes which are formed or enlarged with the greatest rapidity under our eyes cannot be the fruit of honest toil. The really honest workingman, no matter how indefatigable and economical he may be, if he succeeds in raising himself from the state of wage-slave to that of an overseer or contractor, can, by a long life of privations, accumulate at most a few hundreds of dollars. Those who, on the contrary, without making by their own talent industrial discoveries or inventions, accumulate in a few years millions, can be nothing but unscrupulous manipulators of affairs, if we except a few rare strokes of good luck. And it is these very parasites— bankers, etc.,—who live in the most ostentatious luxury enjoying public honors, and holding offices of trust, as a reward for their honorable business methods.

Those who toil, the immense majority, receive barely enough food to keep them from dying of hunger; they live in back-rooms, in garrets, in the filthy alleys of cities, or in the country in hovels not fit for stables for horses or cattle.

Besides all this, we must not forget the horrors of being unable to find work, the saddest and most frequent of the three symptoms of that *equality in misery* which is spreading like a pestilence over the economic world of modern Italy, as indeed, with varying degrees of intensity, it is everywhere else.

I refer to the ever-growing army of the *unemployed* in agriculture and industry—of those who have lost their foothold in the lower middle class,—and of those who have been *expropriated* (robbed) of their little possessions by taxes, debts or usury.

It is not correct, then, to assert that socialism demands for all citizens material and actual equality of labor and rewards.

The only possible equality is equality of obligation to work in order to live, with a guarantee to every laborer of conditions of existence worthy of a human being in exchange for the labor furnished to society.

Equality, according to socialism—as Benoit Malon said[5]—is a relative thing, and must be understood in a two-fold sense: 1st, All men, as men, must be guaranteed human conditions of existence; 2d, All men ought to be equal *at the starting point*, ought not to be handicapped, in the struggle for life, in order that each may freely develop his own personality in an environment of equality of *social* conditions, while to-day a child, sound and healthy, but poor, goes to the wall in competition with a child puny but rich.[6]

This is what constitutes the radical, immeasurable transformation that socialism demands, but that it also has discovered and announces as an evolution—already begun in the world around us—that will be necessarily, inevitably accomplished in the human society of the days to come.[7]

This transformation is summed up in the conversion of private or individual ownership of the means of production, *i. e.* of the physical foundation of human life (land, mines, houses, factories, machinery, instruments of labor or tools, and means of transportation) into collective or social ownership, by means of methods and processes which I will consider further on.

From this point we will consider it as proven that the first objection of the anti-socialist reasoning does not hold, since its starting-point is non-existent. It assumes, in short, that contemporary socialism aims at a chimerical physical and mental equality of all men, when the fact is that scientific and fact-founded socialism never, even in a dream, thought of such a thing.

Socialism maintains, on the contrary, that this inequality—though greatly diminished under a better social organization which will do away with all the physical and mental imperfections that are the cumulative results of generations of poverty and misery—can, nevertheless, never disappear for the reasons that Darwinism has discovered in the mysterious mechanism of life, in other words on account of the principle of variation that manifests itself in the continuous development of species culminating in man.

In every social organization that it is possible to conceive, there will always be some men large and others small, some weak and some strong, some phlegmatic and some nervous, some more intelligent, others less so, some superior in mental power, others in muscular strength; and it is well that it should be so; moreover, it is inevitable.

It is well that this is so, because the variety and inequality of individual aptitudes naturally produce that division of labor that Darwinism has rightly declared to be a law of individual physiology and of social economy.

All men ought to work in order to live, but each ought to devote himself to the kind of labor which best suits his peculiar aptitudes. An injurious waste of strength and abilities would thus be avoided, and labor would cease to be repugnant, and would become agreeable and necessary as a condition of physical and moral health.

And when all have given to society the labor best suited to their innate and acquired aptitudes, each has a right to the same rewards, since each has equally contributed to that solidarity of labor which sustains the life of the social aggregate and, in solidarity with it, the life of each individual.

The peasant who digs the earth performs a kind of labor in appearance more modest, but just as necessary, useful and meritorious as that of the workman who builds a locomotive, of the mechanical engineer who improves it or of the savant who strives to extend the bounds of human knowledge in his study or laboratory.

The one essential thing is that all the members of society work, just as in the individual organism all the cells perform their different functions, more or less modest in appearance—for example, the nerve-cells, the bone-cells or the muscular cells—but all biological functions, or sorts of labor, equally useful and necessary to the life of the organism as a whole.

In the biological organism no living cell remains inactive, and the cell obtains nourishment by material exchanges only in proportion to its labor; in the social organism no individual ought to live without working, whatever form his labor may take.

In this way the majority of the artificial difficulties that our opponents raise against socialism may be swept aside.

"Who, then, will black the boots under the socialist regime?" demands M. Richter in his book so poor in ideas, but which becomes positively grotesque when it assumes that, in the name of social equality the "grand chancellor" of the socialist society will be obliged, before attending to the public business, to black his own boots and mind his own clothes! In truth, if the adversaries of socialism had nothing but arguments of this sort, discussion would indeed be needless.

But all will want to do the least fatiguing and most agreeable kinds of work, says some one with a greater show of seriousness.

I will answer that this is equivalent to demanding to-day the promulgation of a decree as follows: Henceforth all men shall be born painters or surgeons!

The distribution to the proper persons of the different kinds of mental and manual labor will be effected in fact by the anthropological variations in temperament and character, and there will be no need to resort to monkish regulations (another baseless objection to socialism).

Propose to a peasant of average intelligence to devote himself to the study of anatomy or of the penal code or, inversely, tell him whose brain is more highly developed than his muscles to dig the earth, instead of observing with the microscope. They will each prefer the labor for which they feel themselves best fitted.

The changes of occupation or profession will not be as considerable as many imagine when society shall be organized under the collectivist regime. When once the industries ministering to purely *personal* luxury shall be suppressed—luxury which in most cases insults and aggravates the misery of the masses—the quantity and variety of work will adapt themselves gradually, that is to say naturally, to the socialist phase of civilization just as they now conform to the bourgeois phase.

Moreover, under the socialist regime, every one will have the fullest liberty to declare and make manifest his personal aptitudes, and it will not happen, as it does to-day, that many peasants, sons of the people and of the lower middle class, gifted with natural talents, will be compelled to allow their talents to atrophy while they toil as peasants, workingmen or employees, when they would be able to furnish society a different and more fruitful kind of labor, because it would be more in Harmony with their peculiar genius.

The one essential point is this: In exchange for the labor that they furnish to society, society must guarantee to the peasant and the artisan, as well as to the one who devotes himself to the liberal careers, conditions of existence worthy of a human being. Then we will no longer be affronted by the spectacle of a ballet girl, for instance, earning as much in one evening by whirling on her toes as a scientist, a doctor, a lawyer, etc., in a year's work. In fact to-day the latter are in luck if they do that well.

Certainly, the arts will not be neglected under the socialist regime, because socialism wishes life to be agreeable for all, instead of for a privileged few only, as it is to-day; it will, on the contrary, give to all the arts a marvelous impulse, and if it abolishes private luxury this will be all the more favorable to the splendor of the public edifices.

More attention will be paid to assuring to each one remuneration in proportion to the labor performed. This ratio will be ascertained by taking the difficulty and danger of the labor into account and allowing them to reduce the time required for a given compensation. If a peasant in the open air can work seven or eight hours a day, a miner ought not to work more than three or four hours. And, indeed, when everybody shall work, when much unproductive labor shall be suppressed, the aggregate of daily labor to be distributed among men will be much less heavy and more easily endured (by reason of the more abundant food, more comfortable lodging and recreation guaranteed to every worker) than it is to-day by those who toil and who are so poorly paid, and, besides this, the progress of science applied to industry will render human labor less and less toilsome.

Individuals will apply themselves to work, although the wages or remuneration cannot be accumulated as private wealth, because if the normal, healthy, well-fed man avoids excessive or poorly rewarded labor, he does not remain in idleness, since it is a physiological and psychological necessity for him to devote himself to a daily occupation in harmony with his capacities.

The different kinds of sport are for the leisure classes a substitute for productive labor which a physiological necessity imposes upon them, in order that they may escape the detrimental consequences of absolute repose and ennui.

The gravest problem will be to *proportion* the remuneration to the labor of each. You know that collectivism adopts the formula—to each according to his labor, while communism adopts this other—to each according to his needs.

No one can give, in *its practical details*, the solution of this problem; but this impossibility of predicting the future even in its slightest details does not justify those who brand socialism as a utopia incapable of realization. No one could have, *a priori*, in the dawn of any civilization predicted its successive developments, as I will demonstrate when I come to speak of the methods of social renovation.

This is what we are able to affirm with assurance, basing our position on the most certain inductions of psychology and sociology.

It cannot be denied, as Marx himself declared, that this second formula—which makes it possible to distinguish, according to some, anarchy from socialism—represents a more remote and more complex ideal. But it is equally impossible to deny that, in any case, the formula of collectivism represents a phase of social evolution, a period of individual discipline which must necessarily precede communism.[8]

There is no need to believe that socialism will realize in their fulness all the highest possible ideals of humanity and that after its advent there will be nothing left to desire or to battle for! Our descendants would be condemned to idleness and vagabondage if our immediate ideal was so perfect and all-inclusive as to leave them no ideal at which to aim.

The individual or the society which no longer has an ideal to strive toward is dead or about to die.[9] The formula of communism may then be a more remote ideal, when collectivism shall have been completely realized by the historical processes which I will consider further on.

We are now in a position to conclude that there is no contradiction between socialism and Darwinism on the subject of the equality of all men. Socialism has never laid down this proposition and like Darwinism its tendency is toward a better life for individuals and for society.

This enables us also to reply to this objection, too often repeated, that socialism stifles and suppresses human individuality under the leaden pall of collectivism, by subjecting individuals to uniform monastic regulations and by making them into so many human bees in the social honey-comb.

Exactly the opposite of this is true. Is it not obvious that it is under the present bourgeois organization of society that so many individualities atrophy and are lost to humanity, which under other conditions might be developed to their own advantage and to the advantage of society as a whole? To-day, in fact, apart from some rare exceptions, every man is valued for what he *possesses* and not for what he *is*.[10]

He who is born poor, obviously by no fault of his own, may be endowed by Nature with artistic or scientific genius, but if his patrimony is insufficient to enable him to triumph in the first struggles for development and to complete his education, or if he has not, like the shepherd Giotto, the luck to meet with a rich Cimabue, he must inevitably vanish in oblivion in the great prison of wage-slavery, and society itself thus loses treasures of intellectual power.[11]

He who is born rich, although he owes his fortune to no personal exertion, even if his mental capacity is below normal, will play a leading role on the stage of life's theatre, and all servile people will heap praise and flattery upon him, and he will imagine, simply because he *has* money, that he is quite a different person from what in reality he *is*.[12]

When property shall have become collective, that is to say, under the socialist regime, every one will be assured of the means of existence, and the daily labor will simply serve to give free play to the special aptitudes, more or less original, of each individual, and the best and most fruitful (potentially) years of life will not be completely taken up, as they are at present, by the grievous and tragic battle for daily bread.

Socialism will assure to every one a *human* life; it will give each individual true liberty to manifest and develop his or her own physical and intellectual individuality—individualities which they bring into the world at birth and which are infinitely varied and unequal. Socialism does not deny inequality; it merely wishes to utilize this inequality as one of the factors leading to the free, prolific and many-sided development of human life.

FOOTNOTES:

[3] J. De Johannis, *Il concetto dell'equaglianza nel socialismo e nella scienza*, in *Rassegna delle scienza sociali*, Florence, March 15, 1883, and more recently, Huxley, "On the Natural Inequality of Men," in the "Nineteenth Century," January, 1890.

[4] Utopian socialism has bequeathed to us as a mental habit, a habit surviving even in the most intelligent disciples of Marxian socialism, of asserting the existence of certain equalities—the equality of the two sexes, for example—assertions which cannot possibly be maintained.

BEBEL, *Woman in the Past, Present and Future.*

Bebel, the propagandist and expounder of Marxian theories, also repeats this assertion that, from the psycho-physiological point of view, woman is the equal of man, and he attempts to refute, without success, the scientific objections that have been made to this thesis.

Since the scientific investigations of Messrs. Lombroso and Ferrero, embodied in *Donna delinquente, prostituta e normale*, Turin, 1893 (This book has been translated into English, if my memory serves me right.—Tr.), one can no longer deny the physiological and psychological inferiority of woman to man. I have given a Darwinian explanation of this fact (Scuola positiva, 1893, Nos. 7-8), that Lombroso has since completely accepted (*Uomo di genio*, 6e édit, 1894. This book is also available in English, I believe.—Tr.) I pointed out that all the physio-psychical characteristics of woman are the consequences of her great biological function, maternity.

A being who creates another being—not in the fleeting moment of a voluptuous contact, but by the organic and psychical sacrifices of pregnancy, childbirth and giving suck—cannot preserve for herself as much strength, physical and mental, as man whose only function in the reproduction of the species is infinitely less of a drain.

And so, aside from certain individual exceptions, woman has a lower degree of physical sensibility than man (the current opinion is just the opposite), because if her sensibility were greater, she could not, according to the Darwinian law, survive the immense and repeated sacrifices of maternity, and the species would become extinct. Woman's intellect is weaker, especially in synthetic power, precisely because though there are no (Sergi, in *Atti della societa romana di antropologia*, 1894) women of genius, they nevertheless give birth to men of genius.

This is so true that greater sensibility and power of intellect are found in women in whom the function and sentiment of maternity are undeveloped or are only slightly developed (women of genius generally have a masculine physiognomy), and many of them attain their complete intellectual development only after they pass the critical period of life during which the maternal functions cease finally.

But, if it is scientifically certain that woman represents an inferior degree of biological evolution, and that she occupies a station, even as regards her physio-psychical characteristics, midway between the child and the adult male, it does not follow from this that the socialist conclusions concerning the woman question are false.

Quite the contrary. Society ought to place woman, as a human being and as a creatress of men—more worthy therefore of love and respect—in a better juridical and ethical situation than she enjoys at present. Now she is too often a beast of burden or an object of luxury. In the same way when, from the economic point of view, we demand at the present day special measures in behalf of women, we simply take into consideration their special physio-psychical conditions. The present economic individualism exhausts them in factories and rice-fields; socialism, on the contrary, will require from them only such professional, scientific or muscular labor as is in perfect harmony with the sacred function of maternity.

KULISCIOFF, *Il monopolio dell'uomo*, Milan, 1892, 2d edition.—MOZZONI, *I socialisti e l'emancipazione della donna*, Milan, 1891.

[5] B. MALON, *Le Socialisme Integral*, 2 vol., Paris, 1892.

[6] ZULIANI, *Il privilegio della salute*, Milan, 1893.

[7] LETOURNEAU, *Passé, présent et avenir du travail*, in *Revue mensuelle de l'école d'anthropologie*, Paris, June 15, 1894.

[8] M. Zerboglio has very justly pointed out that individualism acting without the pressure of external sanction and by the simple internal impulse toward good (rightness)—this is the distant ideal of Herbert Spencer—can be realized only after a phase of collectivism, during which the individual activity and instincts can be disciplined into social solidarity and weaned from the essentially anarchist individualism of our times when every one, if he is clever enough to "slip through the meshes of the penal code" can do what he pleases without any regard to his fellows.

[9] "Ah, but a man's reach should exceed his grasp," is the way Robert Browning expresses this in "Andrea Del Sarto."—Translator.

[10] Note our common expression: He is worth so much.—Tr.

[11]

"Full many a gem of purest ray serene

    The dark unfathom'd caves of ocean bear:

Full many a flower is born to blush unseen,

    And waste its fragrance on the desert air.

"Some village-Hampden, that with dauntless breast

    The little tyrant of his field withstood,

Some mute inglorious Milton here may rest,

    Some Cromwell, guiltless of his country's blood."

    —Stanzas from GRAY'S "Elegy in a Country Church-yard."—Translator.

[12]

"Cursed be the gold that gilds the straighten'd forehead of the fool!"

    —Tennyson, in "Locksley Hall."

"Gold, yellow, glittering, precious gold!

Thus, much of this will make black, white; foul, fair;

Wrong, right; base, noble; old, young; coward, valiant."

    —Shakespeare, in "Timon of Athens."—Translator.

III.

THE STRUGGLE FOR LIFE AND ITS VICTIMS.

Socialism and Darwinism, it is said, are in conflict on a second point. Darwinism demonstrates that the immense majority—of plants, animals and men—are destined to succumb, because only a small minority triumphs "in the struggle for life"; socialism, on its part, asserts that all ought to triumph and that no one ought to succumb.

It may be replied, in the first place, that, even in the biological domain of the "struggle for existence," the disproportion between the number of individuals who are born and the number of those who survive regularly and progressively grows smaller and smaller as we ascend in the biological scale from vegetables to animals, and from animals to Man.

This law of a decreasing disproportion between the "called" and the "chosen" is supported by the facts even if we limit our observation to the various species belonging to the same natural order. The higher and more complex the organization, the smaller the disproportion.

In fact, in the vegetables, each individual produces every year an infinite number of seeds, and an infinitesimal number of these survive. In the animals, the number of young of each individual diminishes and the number of those who survive continues on the contrary, to increase. Finally, for the human species, the number of individuals that each one can beget is very small and most of them survive.

But, moreover, in the cases of all three, vegetables, animals and men, we find that it is the lower and more simply organized species, the races and classes less advanced in the scale of existence, who reproduce their several kinds with the greatest prolificness and in which generation follows generation most rapidly on account of the brevity of individual life.

A fern produces millions of spores, and its life is very short—while a palm tree produces only a few dozen seeds, and lives a century.

A fish produces several thousand eggs—while the elephant or the chimpanzee have only a few young who live many years.

Within the human species the savage races are the most prolific and their lives are short—while the civilized races have a low birth-rate and live longer.

From all this it follows that, even confining ourselves to the purely biological domain, the number of victors in the struggle for existence constantly tends to approach nearer and nearer to the number of births with the advance or ascent in the biological scale from vegetables to animals, from animals to men, and from the lower species or varieties to the higher species or varieties.

The iron law of "the struggle for existence," then, constantly reduces the number of the victims forming its hecatomb with the ascent of the biological scale, and the rate of decrease becomes more and more rapid as the forms of life become more complex and more perfect.

It would then be a mistake to invoke against socialism the Darwinian law of Natural Selection in the form under which that law manifests itself in the primitive (or lower) forms of life, without taking into account its continuous attenuation as we pass from vegetables to animals, from animals to men, and within humanity itself, from the primitive races to the more advanced races.

And as socialism represents a yet more advanced phase of human progress, it is still less allowable to use as an objection to it such a gross and inaccurate interpretation of the Darwinian law.

It is certain that the opponents of socialism have made a wrong use of the Darwinian law or rather of its "brutal" interpretation in order to justify modern individualist competition which is too often only a disguised form of cannibalism, and which has made the maxim *homo homini lupus* (man to man a wolf; or, freely, "man eats man") the characteristic motto of our era, while Hobbes only made it the ruling principle of the "*state of nature*" of mankind, before the making of the "social contract."

But because a principle has been abused or misused we are not justified in concluding that the principle itself is false. Its abuse often serves as an incentive to define its nature and its limitations more accurately, so that in practice it may be applied more correctly. This will be the result of my demonstration of the perfect harmony that reigns between socialism and Darwinism.

As long ago as the first edition of my work *Socialismo e Criminalità* (pages 179 *et seq.*) I maintained that the struggle for existence is a law immanent in the human race, as it is a law of all living beings, although its forms continually change and though it undergoes more and more attenuation.

This is still the way it appears to me, and consequently, on this point I disagree with some socialists who have thought they could triumph more completely over the objection urged against them in the name of Darwinism by declaring that in human society the "struggle for existence" is a law which is destined to lose all meaning and applicability when the social transformation at which socialism aims shall have been effected.[13]

It is a law which dominates tyrannically all living beings, and it must cease to act and fall inert at the feet of Man, as if he were not merely a link inseparable from the great biological chain!

I maintained, and I still maintain, that the struggle for existence is a law inseparable from life, and consequently from humanity itself, but that, though remaining an inherent and constant law, it is gradually transformed in its essence and attenuated in its forms.

Among primitive mankind the struggle for existence is but slightly differentiated from that which obtains among the other animals. It is the brutal struggle for daily food or for possession of the females—hunger and love are, in fact, the two fundamental needs and the two poles of life—and almost its only method is muscular violence. In a more advanced phase there is joined to this basic struggle the struggle for political supremacy (in the clan, in the tribe, in the village, in the commune, in the State), and, more and more, muscular struggle is superseded by intellectual struggle.

In the historical period the Graeco-Latin society struggled for *civil* equality (the abolition of slavery); it triumphed, but it did not halt, because to live is to struggle; the society of the middle ages struggled for *religious* equality; it won the battle, but it did not halt; and at the end of the last century, it struggled for *political* equality. Must it now halt and remain stationary in the present state of progress? To-day society struggles for *economic* equality, not for an absolute material equality, but for that more practical, truer equality of which I have already spoken. And all the evidence enables us to foresee with mathematical certainty that this victory will be won to give place to new struggles and to new ideals among our descendants.

The successive changes in the subject-matter (or the ideals) of the struggles for existence are accompanied by a progressive mitigation of the methods of combat. Violent and muscular at first, the struggle is becoming, more and more, pacific and intellectual, notwithstanding some atavic recurrences of earlier methods or some psycho-pathological manifestations of individual violence against society and of social violence against individuals.

The remarkable work of Mr. Novicow[14] has recently given a signal confirmation to my opinion, although Novicow has not taken the sexual struggle into account. I will develop my demonstration more fully in the chapter devoted to *l'avenir moral de l'humanité* (the intellectual future of humanity), in the second edition of *Socialismo e Criminalità*.

For the moment I have sufficiently replied to the anti-socialist objection, since I have shown not merely that the disproportion between the number of births and the number of those who survive tends to constantly diminish, but also that the "struggle for existence" itself changes in its essence and grows milder in its processes at each successive phase of the biological and social evolution.

Socialism may then insist that human conditions of existence ought to be guaranteed to all men—in exchange for labor furnished to collective society—without thereby contradicting the Darwinian law of the survival of the victors in the struggle for existence, since this Darwinian law ought to be understood and applied in each of its varying manifestations, in harmony with the law of human progress.

Socialism, scientifically understood, does not deny, and cannot deny, that among mankind there are always some "losers" in the struggle for existence.

This question is more directly connected with the relations which exist between *socialism* and *criminality*, since those who contend that the struggle for existence is a law which does not apply to human society, declare, accordingly, that *crime* (an abnormal and anti-social form of the struggle for life, just as *labor* is its normal and social form) is destined to disappear. Likewise they think they discover a certain contradiction between socialism and the teachings of criminal anthropology concerning the congenital criminal, though these teachings are also deducted from Darwinism.[15]

I reserve this question for fuller treatment elsewhere. Here is in brief my thought as a socialist and as a criminal anthropologist.

In the first place the school of scientific criminologists deal with life as it now is—and undeniably it has the merit of having applied the methods of experimental science to the study of criminal phenomena, of having shown the hypocritical absurdity of modern penal systems based on the notion of free-will and moral delinquency and resulting in the system of cellular confinement, one of the mental aberrations of the nineteenth century, as I have elsewhere qualified it. In its stead the criminologists wish to substitute the simple segregation of individuals who are not fitted for social life on account of pathological conditions, congenital or acquired, permanent or transitory.

In the second place, to contend that socialism will cause the disappearance of all forms of crime is to act upon the impulse of a generous sentiment, but the contention is not supported by a rigorously scientific observation of the facts.

The scientific school of criminology demonstrates that crime is a natural and social phenomenon—like insanity and suicide—determined by the abnormal, organic and psychological constitution of the delinquent and by the influences of the physical and social environment. The anthropological, physical and social factors, all, always, act concurrently in the determination of all offences, the lightest as well as the gravest—as, moreover, they do in the case of all other human actions. What varies in the case of each delinquent and each offense, is the decisive intensity of each order of factors.[16]

For instance, if the case in point is an assassination committed through jealousy or hallucination, it is the anthropological factor which is the most important, although nevertheless consideration must also be paid to the physical environment and the social environment. If it is a question, on the contrary, of crimes against property or even against persons, committed by a riotous mob or induced by alcoholism, etc., it is the social environment which becomes the preponderating factor, though it is, notwithstanding, impossible to deny the influence of the physical environment and of the anthropological factor.

We may repeat the same reasoning—in order to make a complete examination of the objection brought against socialism in the name of Darwinism—on the subject of the ordinary diseases; crime, moreover, is a department of human pathology.

All diseases, acute or chronic, infectious or not infectious, severe or mild, are the product of the anthropological constitution of the individual and of the influence of the physical and social environment. The decisiveness of the personal conditions or of the environment varies in the various diseases; phthisis or heart disease, for instance, depend principally on the organic constitution of the individual, though it is necessary to take the influence of the environment into account; pellagra,[17] cholera, typhus, etc., on the contrary, depend principally on the physical and social conditions of the environment. And so phthisis makes its ravages even among well-to-do people, that is to say, among persons well nourished and well housed, while it is the badly nourished, that is to say, the poor, who furnish the greatest number of victims to pellagra and cholera.

It is, consequently, evident that a socialist regime of collective property which shall assure to every one human conditions of existence, will largely diminish or possibly annihilate—aided by the scientific discoveries and improvement in hygienic measures—the diseases which are principally caused by the conditions of the environment, that is to say by insufficient nourishment or by the want of protection from inclemency of the weather; but we shall not witness the disappearance of the diseases due to traumatic injuries, imprudence, pulmonary affections, etc.

The same conclusions are valid regarding crime. If we suppress poverty and the shocking inequality of economic conditions, hunger, acute and chronic, will no longer serve as a stimulus to crime. Better nourishment will bring about a physical and moral improvement. The abuses of power and of wealth will disappear, and there will be a considerable diminution in the number of crimes due to circumstances (*crimes d'occasion*), crimes caused principally by the social environment. But there are some crimes which will not disappear, such as revolting crimes against decency due to a pathological perversion of the sexual instinct, homicides induced by epilepsy, thefts which result from a psycho-pathological degeneration, etc.

For the same reasons popular education will be more widely diffused, talents of every kind will be able to develop and manifest themselves freely; but this will not cause the disappearance of idiocy and imbecility due to hereditary pathological conditions. Nevertheless it will be possible for different causes to have a preventive and mitigating influence on the various forms of congenital degeneration (ordinary diseases, criminality, insanity and nervous disorders). Among these preventive influences may be: a better economic and social organization, the prudential counsels, constantly growing in efficacy given by experimental biology, and less and less frequent procreation, by means of voluntary abstention, in cases of hereditary disease.

To conclude we will say that, even under the socialist regime—although they will be infinitely fewer—there will always be some who will be vanquished in the struggle for existence—these will be the victims of weakness, of disease, of dissipation, of nervous disorders, of suicide. We may then affirm that socialism does not deny the Darwinian law of the struggle for existence. Socialism will, however, have this indisputable advantage—the epidemic or endemic forms of human degeneracy will be entirely suppressed by the elimination of their principal cause—the physical poverty and (its necessary consequence) the mental suffering of the majority.

Then the struggle for existence, while remaining always the driving power of the life of society, will assume forms less and less brutal and more and more humane. It will become an intellectual struggle. Its ideal of physiological and intellectual progress will constantly grow in grandeur and sublimity when this progressive idealization of the ideal shall be made possible by the guarantee to every one of daily bread for the body and the mind.

The law of the "struggle for life" must not cause us to forget another law of natural and social Darwinian evolution. It is true many socialists have given to this latter law an excessive and exclusive importance, just as some individuals have entirely neglected it. I refer to the law of solidarity which knits together all the living beings of one and the same species—for instance animals who live gregariously in consequence of the abundance of the supply of their common food (herbivorous animals)—or even of different species. When species thus mutually aid each other to live they are called by naturalists *symbiotic* species, and instead of the struggle for life we have co-operation for life.

It is incorrect to state that the struggle for life is the sole sovereign law in Nature and society, just as it is false to contend that this law is wholly inapplicable to human society. The real truth is that even in human society the struggle for life is an eternal law which grows progressively milder in its methods and more elevated in its ideals. But operating concurrently with this we find a law, the influence of which upon the social evolution constantly increases, the law of solidarity or co-operation between living beings.

Even in animal societies mutual aid against the forces of Nature, or against other animals is of constant occurrence, and this is carried much further among human beings, even among savage tribes. One notes this phenomenon especially in tribes which on account of the favorable character of their environment, or because their subsistence is assured and abundant, become of the industrial or peaceful type. The military or warlike type which is unhappily predominant (on account of the uncertainty and insufficiency of subsistence) among primitive mankind and in reactionary phases of civilization, presents us with less frequent examples of it. The industrial type constantly tends, moreover, as Spencer has shown, to take the place of the warlike type.[18]

Confining ourselves to human society alone, we will say that, while in the first stages of the social evolution the law of the struggle for life takes precedence over the law of solidarity, with the growth within the social organism of the division of labor which binds the various parts of the social whole more closely together in inter-dependence, the struggle for life grows milder and is metamorphosed, and the law of co-operation or solidarity gains more and more both in efficiency and in the range of its influence, and this is due to that fundamental reason that Marx pointed out, and which constitutes his great scientific discovery, the reason that in the one case the conditions of existence—food especially—are not assured, and in the other case they are.

In the lives of individuals as in the life of societies, when the means of subsistence, that is to say, the physical basis of existence, are assured, the law of solidarity takes precedence over the law of the struggle for existence, and when they are not assured, the contrary is true. Among savages, infanticide and parricide are not only permitted but are obligatory and sanctioned by religion if the tribe inhabits an island where food is scarce (for instance, in Polynesia), and they are immoral and criminal acts on continents where the food supply is more abundant and certain.[19]

Just so, in our present society, as the majority of individuals are not sure of getting their daily bread, the struggle for life, or "free competition," as the individualists call it, assumes more cruel and more brutal forms.

Just as soon as through collective ownership every individual shall be assured of fitting conditions of existence, the law of solidarity will become preponderant.

When in a family financial affairs run smoothly and prosperously, harmony and mutual good-will prevail; as soon as poverty makes its appearance, discord and struggle ensue. Society as a whole shows us the picture on a large scale. A better social organization will insure universal harmony and mutual good-will.

This will be the achievement of socialism, and, to repeat, for this, the fullest and most fruitful interpretation of the inexorable natural laws discovered by Darwinism, we are indebted to socialism.

FOOTNOTES:

[13] Such socialists are LABUSQUIERE, LANESSAU, LORIA And COLAJANNI.

[14] NOVICOW, *Les luttes entre sociétés, leurs phases successives*, Paris, 1893. LERDA, *La lotta per la vita*, in *Pensiero italiano*, Milan, Feb. and March, 1894.

[15] I regret that M. Loria, ordinarily so profound and acute, has here been deceived by appearances. He has pointed out this pretended contradiction in his "Economic Foundations of Society" (available in English, Tr.). He has been completely answered, in the name of the school of scientific criminal anthropology, by M. RIVIERI DE ROCCHI, *Il diritto penale e un'opera recente di Loria in Scuola positiva nella giurisprudenza penale* of Feb. 15, 1894, and by M. LOMBROSO, in *Archivio di psichiatria e scienza penali*, 1894, XIV, fasc. C.

[16] ENRICO FERRI, Sociologie criminelle (French translation), 1893, Chaps. I. and II.

A recent work has just given scientific confirmation to our inductions: FORSINARI DI VERCE, *Sulla criminalità e le vicende economiche d'Italia dal 1873 al 1890*. Turin, 1894. The preface written by Lombroso concludes in the following words: "We do not wish, therefore, to slight or neglect the truth of the socialist movement, which is destined to changed the current of modern European thought and action, and which contends *ad majorem gloriam* of its conclusions that *all* criminality depends on the influence of the economic environment. We also believe in this doctrine, though we are unwilling and unable to accept the erroneous conclusions drawn from it. However enthusiastic we may be, we will never, in its honor, renounce the truth. We leave this useless servility to the upholders of classical orthodoxy."

[17] A skin-disease endemic in Northern Italy. Tr.

[18] See in this connection the famous monographs of Kropotkin, *Mutual aid among the savages*, in the "Nineteenth Century," April 9, 1891, and *Among the barbarians*, "Nineteenth Century," January, 1892, and also two recent articles signed: "Un Professeur," which appeared in the *Revue Socialiste*, of Paris, May and June, 1894, under the title: *Lutte ou accord pour la vie*.

[19] ENRICO FERRI, *Omicidio nell' antropologia criminale, Introduction*, Turin, 1894.

IV.

THE SURVIVAL OF THE FITTEST.

The third and last part of the argument of Haeckel is correct if applied solely to the purely biological and Darwinian domain, but its starting point is false if it is intended to apply it to the social domain and to turn it into an objection against socialism.

It is said the struggle for existence assures the survival of the fittest; it therefore causes an aristocratic, hierarchic gradation of selected individuals—a continuous progress—and not the democratic leveling of socialism.

Here again, let us begin by accurately ascertaining the nature of this famous natural selection which results from the struggle for existence.

The expression which Haeckel uses and which, moreover, is in current use, "survival of the best or of the best fitted," ought to be corrected. We must suppress the adjective *best*. This is simply a persisting relic of that teleology which used to see in Nature and history a premeditated goal to be reached by means of a process of continuous amelioration or progress.

Darwinism, on the contrary, and still more the theory of universal evolution, has completely banished the notion of final causes from modern scientific thought and from the interpretation of natural phenomena. Evolution consists both of involution and dissolution. It may be true, and indeed it is true, that by comparing the two extremes of the path traversed by humanity we find that there has really been a true progress, an improvement taking it all in all; but, in any case, progress has not followed a straight ascending line, but, as Goethe has said, a spiral with rhythms of progress and of retrogression, of evolution and of dissolution.

Every cycle of evolution, in the individual life as in the collective life, bears within it the germs of the corresponding cycle of dissolution; and, inversely, the latter, by the decay of the form already worn out, prepares in the eternal laboratory new evolutions and new forms of life.

It is thus that in the world of human society every phase of civilization bears within it and is constantly developing the germs of its own dissolution from which issues a new phase of civilization—which will be more or less different from its predecessor in geographical situation and range—in the eternal rhythm of living humanity. The ancient hieratic civilizations of the Orient decay, and through their dissolution they give birth to the Graeco-Roman world, which in turn is followed by the feudal and aristocratic civilization of Central Europe; it also decays and disintegrates through its own excesses, like the preceding civilizations, and it is replaced by the bourgeois civilization which has reached its culminating point in the Anglo-Saxon world. But it is already experiencing the first tremors of the fever of dissolution, while from its womb there emerges and is developing the socialist civilization which will flourish over a vaster domain than that of any of the civilizations which have preceded it.[20]

Hence it is not correct to assert that the natural selection caused by the struggle for existence assures the survival of the *best*; in fact, it assures the survival of the best *fitted*.

This is a very great difference, alike in natural Darwinism and in social Darwinism.

The struggle for existence necessarily causes the survival of the individuals best fitted for the environment and the particular historical period in which they live.

In the natural, biological domain, the free play of natural (*cosmiques*) forces and conditions causes a progressive advance or ascent of living forms, from the microbe up to Man.

In human society, on the contrary, that is to say, in the super-organic evolution of Herbert Spencer, the intervention of other forces and the occurrence of other conditions sometimes causes a retrograde selection which always assures the survival of those who are best fitted for a given environment at a given time, but the controlling principle of this selection is in turn affected by the vicious conditions—if they are vicious—of the environment.

Here we are dealing with the question of "social selection," or rather "social selections," for there is more than one kind of social selection. By starting from this idea—not clearly comprehended—some writers, both socialists and non-socialists, have come to deny that the Darwinian theories have any application to human society.

It is known, indeed, that in the contemporaneous civilized world natural selection is injuriously interfered with by *military* selection, by *matrimonial* selection, and, above all, by *economic* selection.[21]

The temporary celibacy imposed upon soldiers certainly has a deplorable effect upon the human race. It is the young men who on account of comparatively poor physical constitutions are excused from military service, who marry the first, while the healthier individuals are condemned to a transitory sterility, and in the great cities run the risk of contagion from syphilis which unfortunately has permanent effects.

Marriage also, corrupted as it is in the existent society by economic considerations, is ordinarily in practice a sort of retrogressive sexual selection. Women who are true degenerates, but who have good dowries or "prospects," readily find husbands on the marriage market, while the most robust women of the people or of the middle class who have no dowries are condemned to the sterility of compulsory old-maiddom or to surrender themselves to a more or less gilded prostitution.[22]

It is indisputable that the present economic conditions exercise an influence upon all the social relations of men. The monopoly of wealth assures to its possessor the victory in the struggle for existence. Rich people, even though they are less robust, have longer lives than those who are ill-fed. The day-and-night-work, under inhuman conditions, imposed upon grown men, and the still more baleful labor imposed upon women and children by modern capitalism causes a constant deterioration in the biological conditions of the toiling masses.[23]

In addition to all these we must not forget the moral selection—which is really immoral or retrograde—made at present by capitalism in its struggle with the proletariat, and which favors the survival of those with servile characters, while it persecutes and strives to suppress all those who are strong in character, and all who do not seem disposed to tamely submit to the yoke of the present economic order.[24]

The first impression which springs from the recognition of these facts is that the Darwinian law of natural selection does not hold good in human society—in short, is inapplicable to human society.

I have maintained, and I do maintain, on the contrary, in the first place, that these various kinds of retrograde social selection are not in contradiction with the Darwinian law, and that, moreover, they serve as the material for an argument in favor of socialism. Nothing but socialism, in fact, can make this inexorable law of natural selection work more beneficently.

As a matter of fact, the Darwinian law does not cause the "survival of the *best*," but simply the "survival of the *fittest*."

It is obvious that the forms of degeneracy produced by the divers kinds of social selection and notably by the present economic organization merely promote, indeed, and with growing efficiency, the survival of those best fitted for this very economic organization.

If the victors in the struggle for existence are the worst and the weakest, this does not mean that the Darwinian law does not hold good; it means simply that the environment is corrupt (and corrupting), and that those who survive are precisely those who are the fittest for this corrupt environment.

In my studies of criminal psychology I have too often had to recognize the fact that in prisons and in the criminal world it is the most cruel or the most cunning criminals who enjoy the fruits of victory; it is just the same in our modern economic individualist system; the victory goes to him who has the fewest scruples; the struggle for existence favors him who is fittest for a world where a man is valued for what he has (no matter how he got it), and not for what he is.

The Darwinian law of natural selection functions then even in human society. The error of those who deny this proposition springs from the fact that they confound the present environment and the present transitory historical era—which are known in history as the *bourgeois* environment and period, just as the Middle Ages are called *feudal*—with all history and all humanity, and therefore they fail to see that the disastrous effects of modern, retrograde, social selection are only confirmations of the Darwinian law of the "survival of the *fittest*." Popular common sense has long recognized this influence of the surroundings, as is shown by many a common proverb, and its scientific explanation is to be found in the necessary biological relations which exist between a given environment and the individuals who are born, struggle and survive in that environment.

On the other hand, this truth constitutes an unanswerable argument in favor of socialism. By freeing the environment from all the corruptions with which our unbridled economic individualism pollutes it, socialism will necessarily correct the ill effects of natural and social selection. In a physically and morally wholesome environment, the individuals best fitted to it, those who will therefore survive, will be the physically and morally healthy.

In the struggle for existence the victory will then go to him who has the greatest and most prolific physical, intellectual and moral energies. The collectivist economic organization, by assuring to everyone the conditions of existence, will and necessarily must, result in the physical and moral improvement of the human race.

To this some one replies: Suppose we grant that socialism and Darwinian selection may be reconciled, is it not obvious that the survival of the fittest tends to establish an aristocratic gradation of individuals, which is contrary to socialistic leveling?

I have already answered this objection in part by pointing out that socialism will assure to all individuals—instead of as at present only to a privileged few or to society's heroes—freedom to assert and develop their own individualities. Then in truth the result of the struggle for existence will be the survival of the best and this for the very reason that in a wholesome environment the victory is won by the healthiest individuals. Social Darwinism, then, as a continuation and complement of natural (biological) Darwinism, will result in a selection of the best.

To respond fully to this insistence upon an unlimited aristocratic selection, I must call attention to another natural law which serves to complete that rhythm of action and reaction which results in the equilibrium of life.

To the Darwinian law of natural inequalities we must add another law which is inseparable from it, and which Jacoby, following in the track of the labors of Morel, Lucas, Galton, De Caudole, Ribot, Spencer, Royer, Lombroso, and others, has clearly demonstrated and expounded.

This same Nature, which makes "choice" and aristocratic gradation a condition of vital progress, afterwards restores the equilibrium by a leveling and democratic law.

"From the infinite throng of humanity there emerge individuals, families and races which tend to rise above the common level; painfully climbing the steep heights they reach the summits of power, wealth, intelligence and talent, and, having reached the goal, they are hurled down and disappear in the abysses of insanity and degeneration. Death is the great leveler; by destroying every one who rises above the common herd, it democratizes humanity."[25]

Every one who attempts to create a monopoly of natural forces comes into violent conflict with that supreme law of Nature which has given to all living beings the use and disposal of the natural agents: air and light, water and land.

Everybody who is too much above or too much below the average of humanity—an average which rises with the flux of time, but is absolutely fixed at any given moment of history—does not live and disappears from the stage.

The idiot and the man of genius, the starving wretch and the millionaire, the dwarf and the giant, are so many natural or social monsters, and Nature inexorably blasts them with degeneracy or sterility, no matter whether they be the product of the organic life, or the effect of the social organization.

And so, all families possessing a monopoly of any kind—monopoly of power, of wealth or of talent—are inevitably destined to become in their latest offshoots imbeciles, sterile or suicides, and finally to become extinct. Noble houses, dynasties of sovereigns, descendants of millionaires—all follow the common law which, here again, serves to confirm the inductions—in this sense, equalitarian—of science and of socialism.

FOOTNOTES:

[20] One of the most characteristic processes of social dissolution is *parasitism*. MASSART and VANDERVELDE, Parasitism, organic and social. (English translation.) Swan, Sonnenschein & Co., London.

[21] BROCA, *Les sélections* (§ 6. Les sélections sociales) in *Mémoires d' anthropologie*, Paris, 1877, III., 205. LAPOUGE, *Les sélections sociales*, in *Revue d' anthrop.*, 1887, p. 519. LORIA, *Discourse su Carlo Darwin*, SIENNE, 1882. VADALA, *Darwinismo naturale e Darwinismo sociale*, Turin, 1883. BORDIER, *La vie des sociétés*, Paris, 1887. SERGI, *Le degenerazione umane*, Milan, 1889, p. 158. BEBEL, Woman in the past, present and future.

[22] MAX NORDAU, Conventional Lies of our Civilization. (English trans.) Laird & Lee, Chicago, 1895.

[23] While this is shown by all official statistics, it is signally shown by the facts collated by M. Pagliani, the present Director-General of the Bureau of Health in the Interior Department, who has shown that the bodies of the poor are more backward and less developed than those of the rich, and that this difference, though but slightly manifest at birth, becomes greater and greater in after life, *i. e.* as soon as the influence of the economic conditions makes itself felt in all its inexorable tyranny.

[24] TURATI, *Selezione servile*, in *Critica Sociale*, June 1, 1894. SERGI, *Degenerazione umane*, Milan, 1889.

[25] JACOBY, *Etudes sur la sélection dans ses rapports avec l'hérédité chez l'homme*, Paris, 1881, p. 606.

LOMBROSO, *L'uomo di genio*, 6th edition, Turin, 1894, has developed and complemented this law. This law, so easily forgotten, is neglected by RITCHIE (Darwinism and Politics. London. Sonnenschein, 1891.) in the section called "Does the doctrine of Heredity support Aristocracy?"

V.

SOCIALISM AND RELIGIOUS BELIEFS.

Not one of the three contradictions between socialism and Darwinism, which Haeckel formulated, and which so many others have echoed since, resists a candid and more accurate examination of the natural laws which bear the name of Charles Darwin.

I add that not only is Darwinism not in contradiction with socialism, but that it constitutes one of its fundamental scientific premises. As Virchow justly remarked, socialism is nothing but a logical and vital corollary, in part of Darwinism, in part of Spencerian evolution.

The theory of Darwin, whether we wish it or not, by demonstrating that man is descended from the animals, has dealt a severe blow to the belief in God as the creator of the universe and of man by a special *fiat*. This, moreover, is why the most bitter opposition, and the only opposition which still continues, to its scientific inductions, was made and is made in the name of religion.

It is true that Darwin did not declare himself an atheist[26] and that Spencer is not one; it is also true that, strictly speaking, the theory of Darwin, like that of Spencer, can also be reconciled with the belief in God, since it may be admitted that God created matter and force, and that both afterward evolved into their successive forms in accordance with the initial creative impulse. Nevertheless, it cannot be denied that these theories, by rendering the idea of causality more and more inflexible and universal, lead necessarily to the negation of God, since there always remains this question: And God, who created him? And if it is replied that God has always existed, the same reply may be flung back by asserting that the universe has always existed. To use the phrase of Ardigò, human thought is only able to conceive the chain which binds effects to causes as terminating at a given point, purely conventional.[27]

God, as Laplace said, is an hypothesis of which exact science has no need; he is, according to Herzen, at the most an X, which represents not the *unknowable*—as Spencer and Dubois Raymond contend—but all that which humanity does not yet know. Therefore, it is a variable X which decreases in direct ratio to the progress of the discoveries of science.

It is for this very reason that science and religion are in inverse ratio to each other; the one diminishes and grows weaker in the same proportion that the other increases and grows stronger in its struggle against the unknown.[28]

And if this is one of the consequences of Darwinism, its influence on the development of socialism is quite obvious.

The disappearance of faith in the hereafter, where the poor shall become the elect of the Lord, and where the miseries of the "vale of tears" will find an eternal compensation in paradise, gives greater strength to the desire for some semblance of an "earthly paradise" here below even for the unfortunate and the poor, who are the great majority.

Hartmann and Guyau[29] have shown that the evolution of religious beliefs may be summarized thus: All religions include, with various other matters, the promise of happiness; but the primitive religions concede that this happiness will be realized during the life of the individual himself, and the later religions, through an excess of reaction, place its realization after death, outside the human world; in the final phase, this realization of happiness is once more placed within the field of human life, no longer in the ephemeral moment of the individual existence, but indeed in the continuous evolution of all mankind.

On this side, then, socialism is closely related to the religious evolution, and tends to substitute itself for religion, since its aim is for humanity to have its own "earthly paradise" here, without having to wait for it in the *hereafter*, which, to say the least, is very problematical.

Therefore, it has been very justly remarked that the socialist movement has many traits in common with, for example, primitive Christianity, notably that ardent faith in the ideal that has definitively deserted the arid field of bourgeois skepticism, and some savants, not socialists, such as Messrs. Wallace, de Lavaleye and the Roberty, etc., admit that it is entirely possible for socialism to replace by its humanitarian faith the faith in the hereafter of the former religions.

More direct and potent than these relations (between socialism and faith in a hereafter) are, however, the relations which exist between socialism and the belief in God.

It is true that Marxian Socialism, since the Congress held at Erfurt (1891), has rightly declared that religious beliefs are private affairs[30] and that, therefore, the Socialist party combats religious intolerance under all its forms, whether it be directed against Catholics[31] or against Jews, as I have shown in an article against *Anti-Semitism*.[32] But this breadth of superiority of view is, at bottom, only a consequence of the confidence in final victory.

It is because socialism knows and foresees that religious beliefs, whether one regards them, with Sergi,[33] as pathological phenomena of human psychology, or as useless phenomena of moral incrustation, are destined to perish by atrophy with the extension of even elementary scientific culture. This is why socialism does not feel the necessity of waging a special warfare against these religious beliefs which are destined to disappear. It has assumed this attitude although it knows that the absence or the impairment of the belief in God is one of the most powerful factors for its extension, because the priests of all religions have been, throughout all the phases of history, the most potent allies of the ruling classes in keeping the masses pliant and submissive under the yoke by means of the enchantment of religion, just as the tamer keeps wild beasts submissive by the terrors of the cracks of his whip.

And this is so true that the most clear-sighted conservatives, even though they are atheists, regret that the religious sentiment—that precious narcotic—is diminishing among the masses, because they see in it, though their pharisaism does not permit them to say it openly, an instrument of political domination.[34]

Unfortunately, or fortunately, the religious sentiment cannot be re-established by royal decree. If it is disappearing, the blame for this cannot be laid at the door of any particular individual, and there is no need of a special propaganda against it, because its antidote impregnates the air we breathe—saturated with the inductions of experimental science—and religion no longer meets with conditions favorable to its development as it did amid the superstitious ignorance of past centuries.

I have thus shown the direct influence of modern science, science based on observation and experiment,—which has substituted the idea of natural causality for the ideas of miracle and divinity,—on the extremely rapid development and on the experimental foundation of contemporary socialism.

Democratic socialism does not look with unfriendly eyes upon "Catholic Socialism" (the Christian Socialism of Southern Europe), since it has nothing to fear from it.

Catholic socialism, in fact, aids in the propagation of socialist ideas, especially in the rural districts where religious faith and practices are still very vigorous, but it will not win and wear the palm of victory *ad majorem dei gloriam*. As I have shown, there is a growing antagonism between science and religion, and the socialist varnish cannot preserve Catholicism. The "earthly" socialism has, moreover, a much greater attractive power.

When the peasants shall have become familiar with the views of Catholic socialism, it will be very easy for democratic socialism to rally them under its own flag—they will, indeed, convert themselves.

Socialism occupies an analogous position with regard to republicanism. Just as atheism is a private affair which concerns the individual conscience, so a republican form of government is a private affair which interests only a part of the bourgeoisie. Certainly, by the time that socialism draws near to its day of triumph, atheism will have made immense progress, and a republican form of government will have been established in many countries which to-day submit to a monarchical regime. But it is not socialism which develops atheism, any more than it is socialism which will establish republicanism. Atheism is a product of the theories of Darwin and Spencer in the present bourgeois civilization, and republicanism has been and will be, in the various countries, the work of a portion of the capitalist bourgeoisie, as was recently said in some of the conservative newspapers of Milan (*Corriere della sera* and *Idea liberale*), when "the monarchy shall no longer serve the interests of the country," that is to say of the class in power.

The evolution from absolute monarchy to constitutional monarchy and to republicanism is an obvious historical law; in the present phase of civilization the only difference between the two latter is in the elective or hereditary character of the head of the State. In the various countries of Europe, the bourgeoisie themselves Hill demand the transition from monarchy to republicanism, in order to put off as long as possible the triumph of socialism. In Italy as in France, in England as in Spain, we see only too many republicans or "radicals" whose attitude with regard to social questions is more bourgeois and more conservative than that of the intelligent conservatives. At Montecitorio, for example, there is Imbriani whose opinions on religious and social matters are more conservative than those of M. di Rudini. Imbriani, whose personality is moreover very attractive, has never attacked the priests or monks—this man who attacks the entire universe and very often with good reason, although without much success on account of mistaken methods—and he was the only one to oppose even the consideration of a law proposed by the *Député* Ferrari, which increased the tax on estates inherited by collateral heirs!

Socialism then has no more interest in preaching republicanism than it has in preaching atheism. To each his role (or task), is the law of division of labor. The struggle for atheism is the business of science; the establishment of republicanism in the various countries of Europe has been and will be the work of the bourgeoisie themselves—whether they be conservative or radical. All this constitutes the historical progress toward socialism, and individuals are powerless to prevent or delay the succession of the phases of the moral, political and social evolution.

FOOTNOTES:

[26] Darwin never made a declaration of atheism, but that was in fact his way of looking at the problem ("*sa manière de voir.*").

While Haeckel, concerned solely with triumphing over the opposition, said at the Congress of Eisenach (1882) that Darwin was not an atheist, Büchner, on the contrary, published shortly afterward a letter which Darwin had written him, and in which he avowed that "since the age of forty years, his scientific studies had led him to atheism."

(See also, "Charles Darwin and Karl Marx: A Comparison," by Ed. Aveling. Published by the Twentieth Century Press, London.—Translator.)

In the same way, John Stuart Mill never declared himself a Socialist, but that, nevertheless, in opinion he was one, is made evident by his autobiography and his posthumous fragments on Socialism. (See "The Socialism of John Stuart Mill." Humboldt Pub. Co., New York.—Tr.)

[27] ARDIGÒ, *La Formazione naturale*, Vol. II. of his *Opere filologiche*, and Vol. VI., *La Ragione*, Padone, 1894.

[28] Guyau, *L'Irréligion de l'avenir.* Paris. 1887.

[29] The dominant factor, nevertheless, in religious beliefs, is the hereditary or traditional *sentimental* factor; this it is which always renders them respectable when they are professed in good faith, and often makes them even appeal to our sympathies,—and this is precisely because of the ingenuous or refined sensibility of the persons in whom religious faith is the most vital and sincere.

[30] NITTI, *Le Socialisme catholique*, Paris, 1894, p. 27 and 393.

[31] Its usual form in America.—Translator.

[32] *Nuova Rassegna*, August, 1894.

[33] SERGI, *L'origine dei fenomeni psichici e loro significazione biologica*, Milan, 1885, p. 334, *et seq.*

[34] DURKHEIM, *De la division du travail social.* Paris. 1893. As regards the pretended influence of religion on personal morality I have shown how very slight a foundation there was for this opinion in my studies on criminal psychology, and more particularly in *Omicidio nell' antropologia criminale.*

VI.

THE INDIVIDUAL AND THE SPECIES.

It can also be shown that scientific socialism proceeds directly from Darwinism by an examination of the different modes of conceiving of the individual in relation to the species.

The eighteenth century closed with the exclusive glorification of the individual, of the *man*—as an entity in himself. In the works of Rousseau this was only a beneficent, though exaggerated re-action against the political and sacerdotal tyranny of the Middle Ages.

This individualism led directly to that artificiality in politics, which I will consider a little further on in studying the relations between the theory of evolution and socialism, and which is common to the ruling classes under the bourgeois regime and to the individualistic anarchists,—since both alike imagine that the social organization can be changed in a day by the magical effect of a bomb,—more or less murderous.

Modern biology has radically changed this conception of the *individual* and it has demonstrated, in the domain of biology as in that of sociology, that the individual is himself only an aggregation of more simple living elements, and likewise that the individual in himself, the *Selbstwesen* of the Germans, does not exist in independent isolation, but only as a member of a society (*Gliedwesen*).

Every living object is an association, a collectivity.

The monad itself, the living cell, the irreducible expression of biological individuality, is also an aggregate of various parts (nucleus, *nucléole*, protoplasm), and each one of them in its turn is an aggregate of molecules which are aggregates of atoms.

The atom does not exist alone, as an individual; the atom is invisible and impalpable and it does not live.

And the complexity of the aggregation, the federation of the parts constantly increases with the ascent in the zoological series from protozoa to Man.

Unifying, Jacobin artificiality corresponds to the metaphysics of individualism, just as the conception of national and international federalism corresponds to the scientific character of modern socialism.

The organism of a mammal is simply a federation of tissues, organs and anatomical machinery; the organism of a society can consist of nothing but a federation of communes, provinces and regions; the organism of humanity can be nothing but a federation of nations.

If it is absurd to conceive of a mammal whose head should have to move in the same fashion as the extremities and all of whose extremities would have to perform the same motions simultaneously, there is no less absurdity in a political and administrative organization in which the extreme northern province or the mountainous province, for instance, have to have the same bureaucratic machinery, the same body of laws, the same methods, etc., as the extreme southern province or the province made up of plains, solely through the passion for symmetrical uniformity, that pathological expression of unity.

If we disregard those considerations of a political order which make it possible to conclude, as I have done elsewhere,[35] that the only possible organization for Italy, as for every other country, appeared to me to be that of an administrative federalism combined with political unity, we can regard it as manifest, that at the close of the nineteenth century the individual, as an independent entity, is dethroned alike in biology and sociology.

The individual exists, but only in so far as he forms a part of a social aggregate.

Robinson Crusoe—that perfect type of individualism—can not possibly be aught but a legend or a pathological specimen.

The species—that is to say, the social aggregate—is the great, the living and eternal reality of life, as has been demonstrated by Darwinism and confirmed by all the inductive sciences from astronomy to sociology.

At the close of the eighteenth century Rousseau thought that the individual alone existed, and that society was an artificial product of the "social contract" and, as he attributed (just as Aristotle had done in the case of slavery) a permanent human character to the transitory manifestations of the period, such as the rottenness of the regime under which he lived, he further thought that Society was the cause of all evils, and that individuals are all born good and equal. At the end of the nineteenth century, on the contrary, all the inductive sciences agree in recognizing that society, the social aggregate, is a fact of Nature, inseparable from life, in the vegetable species as in the animal species, from the lowest "animal colonies" of zoophytes up to societies of mammals (herbivora), and to human society.[36]

All that is best in the individual, he owes to the social life, although every phase of evolution is marked at its decline by pathological conditions of social decay—essentially transitory, however—which inevitably precede a new cycle of social renovation.

The individual, as such, if he could live, would fulfill only one of the two fundamental requirements (needs) of existence: alimentation—that is to say, the selfish preservation of his own organism, by means of that primordial and fundamental function, which Aristotle designated by the name of *ctesi*—the conquest of food.

But all individuals have to live in society because a second fundamental requirement of life imposes itself upon the individual, *viz.*, the reproduction of beings like himself for the preservation of the species. It is this life of relationship and reproduction (sexual and social) which gives birth to the moral or social sense, which enables the individual not only *to be, but to co-exist with his fellows.*

It may be said that these two fundamental instincts of life—bread and love—by their functioning maintain a social equilibrium in the life of animals, and especially in Man.

It is love which causes, in the great majority of men, the principal physiological and psychical expenditure of the forces accumulated in larger or smaller quantities by the consumption of daily bread, and which the daily labor has not absorbed or which parasitic inaction has left intact.

Even more—love is the only pleasure which truly has a universal and equalitarian character. The people have named it "the paradise of the poor;" and religions have always bidden them to enjoy it without limits—"be fruitful and multiply"—because the erotic exhaustion which results from it, especially in males, diminishes or hides beneath the pall of forgetfulness the tortures of hunger and servile labor, and permanently enervates the energy of the individual; and to this extent it performs a function useful to the ruling class.

But indissolubly linked to this effect of the sexual instinct there is an other, the increase of the population. Hence it happens that the desire to eternize a given social order is thwarted and defeated by the pressure of this population which in our epoch assumes the characteristic form of the *proletariat,*—and the social evolution continues its inexorable and inevitable forward march.

It follows from our discussion that while at the end of the eighteenth century it was thought that Society was made for the individual—and from that the deduction could be made that millions of individuals could and ought to toil and suffer for the exclusive advantage of a few individuals—at the end of our century the inductive sciences have demonstrated, just the opposite, that it is the individual who lives for the species and that the latter is the only eternal reality of life.

There we have the starting-point of the sociological or socialist tendency of modern scientific thought in the face of the exaggerated individualism inherited from the last century.

Modern biology also demonstrates that it is necessary to avoid the opposite excess—into which certain schools of utopian socialism and of communism fall—the excess of regarding only the interests of Society and altogether neglecting the individual. An other biological law shows us, in fact, that the existence of the aggregation is the resultant of the life of all the individuals, just as the existence of an individual is the resultant of the life of its constituent cells.

We have demonstrated that the socialism which characterizes the end of the nineteenth century and which will illumine the dawn of the coming century is in perfect harmony with the entire current of modern thought. This harmony manifests itself even on the fundamental question of the predominance given to the vital necessity of collective or social solidarity over the dogmatic exaggerations of individualism, and if the latter at the close of the last century was the outward sign of a potent and fruitful awakening, it inevitably leads, through the pathological manifestations of unbridled competition, to the "libertarian" explosions of anarchism which preaches "individual action," and which is entirely oblivious of human and social solidarity.

We now come to the last point of contact and essential oneness that there is between Darwinism and socialism.

FOOTNOTES:

[35] *Sociologie criminelle*, French trans., Paris, 1892.

[36] I cannot consider here the recent attempt at eclecticism made by M. Fouillée and others. M. Fouillée wishes to oppose, or at least to add, to the *naturalistic* conception of society the consensual or *contractual* conception. Evidently, since no theory is absolutely false, there is even in this consensual theory a share of truth, and the liberty of emigration may be an instance of it—as long as this liberty is compatible with the economic interests of the class in power. But, obviously, this consent, which does not exist at the birth of each individual into such or such a society (and this fact of birth is the most decisive and tyrannical factor in life) also has very little to do with the development of his aptitudes and tendencies, dominated as they are by the iron law of the economic and political organization in which he is an atom.

VIII.

THE "STRUGGLE FOR LIFE" AND THE "CLASS-STRUGGLE."

Darwinism has demonstrated that the entire mechanism of animal evolution may be reduced to the struggle for existence between individuals of the same species on the one hand, and between each species and the whole world of living beings.

In the same way all the machinery of social evolution has been reduced by Marxian socialism to the law of the *Struggle between Classes*. This theory not only gives us the secret motive-power and the only scientific explanation of the history of mankind; it also furnishes the ideal and rigid standard of discipline for political socialism and thus enables it to avoid all the elastic, vaporous, inconclusive uncertainties of sentimental socialism.

The only scientific explanation of the history of animal life is to be found in the grand Darwinian law of the *struggle for existence*; it alone enables us to determine the natural causes of the appearance, development and disappearance of vegetable and animal species from paleontological times down to our own day. In the same way the only explanation of the history of human life is to be found in the grand Marxian law of the *struggle between classes*; thanks to it the annals of primitive, barbarous and civilized humanity cease to be a capricious and superficial kaleidoscopic arrangement of individual episodes in order to become a grand and inevitable drama, determined—whether the actors realize it or not, in its smallest internal details as well as in its catastrophes—by the *economic conditions*, which form the indispensable, physical basis of life and by the *struggle between the classes* to obtain and keep control of the economic forces, upon which all the others—political, juridical and moral—necessarily depend.

I will have occasion to speak more at length—in studying the relations between sociology and socialism—of this grand conception, which is the imperishable glory of Marx and which assures him in sociology the place which Darwin occupies in biology and Spencer in philosophy.[37]

For the moment it suffices for me to point out this new point of contact between Socialism and Darwinism. The expression, *Class-Struggle*, so repugnant when first heard or seen (and I confess that it produced this impression on me when I had not yet grasped the scientific import of the Marxian theory), furnishes us, if it be correctly understood, the primary law of human history and, therefore, it alone can give us the certain index of the advent of the new phase of evolution which Socialism foresees and which it strives to hasten.

To assert the existence of the class-struggle is equivalent to saying that human society, like all other living organisms, is not a homogeneous whole, the sum of a greater or smaller number of individuals; it is, on the contrary, a living organism which is made up of diverse parts, and their differentiation constantly increases in direct ratio to the degree of social evolution attained.

Just as a protozoon is almost wholly composed of albuminoid gelatine, while a mammal is composed of tissues widely varying in kind, in the same way a tribe of primitive savages, without a chief, is composed simply of a few families and the aggregation is the result of mere material propinquity, while a civilized society of the historical or contemporaneous period is made up of social classes which differ, the one from the other, either through the physio-psychical constitutions of their component members, or through the whole of their customs and tendencies, and their personal, family or social life.

These different classes may be rigorously separated. In ancient India they range from the *brahman* to the *sudra*: in the Europe of the Middle Ages, from the Emperor and the Pope to the feudatory and the vassal, down to the artisan, and an individual cannot pass from one class into another, as his social condition is determined solely by the hazard of birth. Classes may lose their legal character, as happened in Europe and America after the French Revolution, and exceptionally there may be an instance of an individual passing from one class into another, analogously to the endosmose and exosmose of molecules, or, to use the phrase of M. Dumont, by a sort of "social capillarity." But, in any case, these different classes exist as an assured reality and they resist every juridical attempt at leveling as long as the fundamental reason for their differentiation remains.

It is Karl Marx who, better than any one else, has proved the truth of this theory by the mass of sociological observations which he has drawn from societies under the most diverse economic conditions.

The names (of the classes), the circumstances and phenomena of their hostile contact and conflict may vary with the varying phases of social evolution, but the tragic essence of history always appears in the antagonism between those who hold the monopoly of the means of production—and these are few—and those who have been robbed (expropriated) of them—and these are the great majority.

Warriors and *shepherds* in the primitive societies, as soon as first, family and then individual ownership of land has superseded the primitive collectivism; *patricians* and *plebeians*—*feudatories* and *vassals*—*nobles* and *common people*—*bourgeoisie* and *proletariat*; these are so many manifestations of one and the same fact—the monopoly of wealth on one side, and productive labor on the other.

Now, the great importance of the Marxian law—the struggle between classes—consists principally in the fact that it indicates with great exactness *just what* is in truth the vital point of the social question and *by what method* its solution may be reached.

As long as no one had shown on positive evidence the economic basis of the political, juridical and moral life, the aspirations of the great majority for the amelioration of social conditions aimed vaguely at the demand and the partial conquest of some *accessory* instrumentality, such as freedom of worship, political suffrage, public education, etc. And certainly, I have no desire to deny the great utility of these conquests.

But the *sancta sanctorum* always remained impenetrable to the eyes of the masses, and as economic power continued to be the privilege of a few, all the conquests and all the concessions had no real basis, separated, as they were, from the solid and fecund foundation which alone can give life and abiding power.

Now, that Socialism has shown—even before Marx, but never before with so much scientific precision—that individual ownership, private property in land and the means of production is the vital point of the question—the problem is formulated in exact terms in the consciousness of contemporaneous humanity.

What method will it be necessary to employ in order to abolish this monopoly of economic power, and the mass of suffering and ills, of hate and injustice which flow from it?

The method of the *Class Struggle*, based on the scientifically proven fact that every class tends to preserve and increase its acquired advantages and privileges, teaches the class deprived of economic power that in order to succeed in conquering it, the struggle (we will consider, further on, the forms of this struggle) must be a struggle of class against class, and not of individual against individual.

Hatred toward such or such an individual—even if it result in his death—does not advance us a single step toward the solution of the problem; it rather retards its solution, because it provokes a reaction in the general feeling against personal violence and it violates the principle of *respect for the human person* which socialism proclaims most emphatically for the benefit of all and against all opponents. The solution of the problem does not become easier because it is recognized that the present abnormal condition, which is becoming more and more acute—misery for the masses and pleasure for a few—is not the consequence of the bad intentions of such or such an individual.

Viewed from this side also socialism is, in fact, in perfect harmony with modern science, which denies the free will of man and sees in human activity, individual and collective, a necessary effect whose determining causes are the conditions of race and environment, acting concurrently.[38]

Crime, suicide, insanity, misery are not the fruits of free will, of individual faults, as metaphysical spiritualism believes, and neither is it an effect of free will, a fault of the individual capitalist if the workingman is badly paid, if he is without work, if he is poor and miserable.

All social phenomena are the necessary resultants of the historical conditions and of the environment. In the modern world the facility and the greater frequency of communication and relations of every kind between all parts of the earth have also increased the dependence of every fact—economic, political, juridical, ethical, artistic or scientific—upon the most remote and apparently unrelated conditions of the life of the great world.

The present organization of private property with no restrictions upon the right of inheritance by descent or upon personal accumulation; the ever increasing and more perfect application of scientific discoveries to the facilitation of human labor—the labor of adapting the materials furnished by Nature to human needs; the telegraph and the steam-engine, the constantly overflowing torrent of human migrations—all these bind, with invisible but infrangible threads, the existence of a family of peasants, work-people or petty trades-people to the life of the whole world. And the harvest of coffee, cotton or wheat in the most distant countries makes its effects felt in all parts of the civilized world, just as the decrease or increase of the sun-spots are phenomena co-incident with the periodical agricultural crises and have a direct influence on the destinies of millions of men.

This magnificent scientific conception of the "unity of physical forces," to use the expression of P. Secchi, or of universal solidarity is far, indeed, from that infantile conception which finds the causes of human phenomena in the free wills of individuals.

If a socialist were to attempt, even for philanthropic purposes, to establish a factory in order to give work to the unemployed, and if he were to produce articles out of fashion or for which there was no general demand, he would soon become bankrupt in spite of his philanthropic intentions by an inevitable effect of inexorable economic laws.

Or, again, if a socialist should give the laborers in his establishment wages two or three times as high as the current rate of wages, he would evidently have the same fate, since he would be dominated by the same economic laws, and he would have to sell his commodities at a loss or keep them unsold in his warehouses, because his prices for the same qualities of goods would be above the market price.

He would be declared a bankrupt and the only consolation the world would offer him would be to call him an *honest man* (*brave homme*); and in the present phase of "mercantile ethics" we know what this expression means.[39]

Therefore, without regard to the personal relations, more or less cordial, between capitalists and workingmen, their respective economic situations are inexorably determined by the present (industrial) organization, in accordance with the law of surplus-labor which enabled Marx to explain and demonstrate irrefutably how the capitalist is able to accumulate wealth without working,—because the laborer produces in his day's work an amount of wealth exceeding in value the wage he receives, and this surplus-product forms the gratuitous (unearned) profit of the capitalist. Even if we deduct from the total profits his pay for technical and administrative superintendence, this unearned surplus-product still remains.

Land, abandoned to the sun and the rain, does not, of itself, produce either wheat or wine. Minerals do not come forth, unaided, from the bowels of the earth. A bag of dollars shut up in a safe does not produce dollars, as a cow produces calves.

The production of wealth results only from a transformation of (Nature-given) materials effected by human labor. And it is only because the peasant tills the land, because the miner extracts minerals, because the laborer sets machinery in motion, because the chemist makes experiments in his laboratory, because the engineer invents machinery, etc., that the capitalist or the landlord—though the wealth inherited from his father may have cost him no labor, and though he may practise *absenteeism* and thus make no personal exertion—is able every year to enjoy riches that others have produced for him, in exchange for wretched lodgings and inadequate nourishment—while the workers are, in most cases, poisoned by the miasmatic vapors from rivers or marshes, by gas in mines and by dust in factories—in brief, in exchange for wages which are always inadequate, to assure the workers conditions of existence worthy of human creatures.

Even under a system of absolute *métayage* (share-farming)—which has been called a form of practical socialism—we always have this question left unanswered. By what miracle does the landlord, who does not work, get his barns and houses filled with wheat and oil and wine in sufficient quantities to enable him to live in ample comfort, while the *métayer* (the tenant on shares) is obliged to work every day, in order to wrest from the earth enough to support himself and his family in wretchedness?

And the system of *métayage* does at least give the tenant the tranquillizing assurance that he will reach the end of the year without experiencing all the horrors of enforced idleness to which the ordinary day or wage laborers are condemned in both city and country. But, in substance, the whole problem in its entirety remains unsolved (even under this system), and there is always one man who lives in comfort, without working, because ten others live poorly by working.[40]

This is the way the system of private property works, and these are the consequences it produces, without any regard to the wills or wishes of individuals.

Therefore, every attempt made against such or such an individual is condemned to remain barren of results; it is the ruling tendency of Society, the objective point which must be changed, it is private ownership which must be abolished, not by a *partition* ("dividing up"), which would result in the most extreme and pernicious form of private ownership, since by the end of a year the persistence of the old individualist principle would restore the *status quo ante*, and all the advantage would accrue solely to the most crafty and the least scrupulous.

Our aim must be the abolition of private ownership and the establishment of collective and social ownership in land and the means of production. This substitution cannot be the subject for a decree,—though the intention to effect it by a decree is attributed to us—but it is in course of accomplishment under our eyes, every day, from hour to hour, directly or indirectly.

Directly, because civilization shows us the continuous substitution of public ownership and social functions for private ownership and individual functions. Roads, postal systems, railways, museums, city lighting-plants, water-plants, schools, etc., which were only a few years since private properties and functions, have become social properties and functions. And it would be absurd to imagine that this direct process of socialization is destined to come to a halt to-day, instead of becoming progressively more and more marked, in accordance with every tendency of our modern life.

Indirectly, since it is the outcome toward which the economic individualism of the bourgeoisie tends. The bourgeois class, which takes its name from the dwellers in the *bourgs* (towns) which the feudal chateau and the Church—symbols of the class then dominant—protected, is the result of fecund labor intelligently directed toward its goal and of historical conditions which have changed the economic structure and tendency of the world (the discovery of America, for instance). This class achieved its revolution in the end of the eighteenth century, and conquered the political power. In the history of the civilized world, it has inscribed a page in letters of gold by those wondrous developments in the lives of nations that are truly epic in character, and by its marvelous applications of science to industry ... but it is now traversing the downward branch of the parabola, and symptoms are appearing which announce to us—and offer proof of their announcement—its dissolution; without its disappearance, moreover, the advent and establishment of a new social phase would be impossible.

Economic individualism carried out to its ultimate logical consequences, necessarily causes the progressive multiplication of property in hands of a constantly diminishing number of persons. *Milliardaire* (billionaire) is a new word, which is characteristic of the nineteenth century, and this new word serves to express and emphasize that phenomenon—in which Henry George saw the historic law of individualism—of the rich becoming richer while the poor become poorer.[41]

Now it is evident that the smaller is the number of those who hold possession of the land and the means of production the easier is their expropriation—with or without indemnification—for the benefit of a single proprietor which is and can be Society alone.

Land is the physical basis of the social organism. It is then absurd for it to belong to a few and not to the whole social collectivity; it would not be any more absurd for the air we breathe to be the monopoly of a few *airlords*.

That (the socialization of the land and the means of production) is truly the supreme goal of socialism, but evidently it can not be reached by attacking such or such a landlord, or such or such a capitalist. The individualist mode of conflict is destined to remain barren of results, or, to say the least, it requires a terribly extravagant expenditure of strength and efforts to obtain merely partial or provisional results.

And so those politicians, whose conception of statesmanship is a career of daily, trivial protests, who see nothing in politics but a struggle between individuals—and those tactics no longer produce any effect either on the public or on legislative assemblies, because they have at last become wonted to them—produce just about as much effect as would fantastic champions of hygiene who should attempt to render a marsh inhabitable by killing the mosquitoes one by one with shots from a revolver, instead of adopting as their method and their goal the draining of the pestilential marsh.

No individual conflicts, no personal violence, but a Class Struggle. It is necessary to make the immense army of workers of all trades and of all professions conscious of these fundamental truths. It is necessary to show them that their class interests are in opposition to the interests of the class who possess the economic power, and that it is by class-conscious organization that they will conquer this economic power through the instrumentality of the other public powers that modern civilization has assured to free peoples. It may, nevertheless, be foreseen that, in every country, the ruling class, before yielding, will abridge or destroy even these public liberties which were without danger for them when they were in the hands of laborers not organized into a class-conscious party, but forming the rearguard of other purely political parties, as radical on secondary questions as they are profoundly conservative on the fundamental question of the economic organization of property.

A Class-Struggle, therefore a struggle of class against class; and a struggle (this is understood), by the methods of which I will soon speak in discussing the four modes of social transformation: evolution— revolution—rebellion—individual violence. But a Class-Struggle in the Darwinian sense, which renews in the history of Man the magnificent drama of the struggle for life between species, instead of degrading us to the savage and meaningless brute strife of individual with individual.

We can stop here. The examination of the relations between Darwinism and socialism might lead us much further, but it would go on constantly eliminating the pretended contradiction between the two currents of modern scientific thought, and it would, on the contrary, confirm the essential, natural and indissoluble harmony that there is between them.

Thus the penetrating view of Virchow is confirmed by that of Leopold Jacoby.

"The same year in which appeared Darwin's book (1859) and coming from a quite different direction, an identical impulse was given to a very important development of social science by a work which long passed unnoticed, and which bore the title: *Critique de l'économie politique* by KARL MARX—it was the forerunner of *Capital*.

"What Darwin's book on the *Origin of Species* is on the subject of the genesis and evolution of organic life from non-sentient nature up to Man, the work of Marx is on the subject of the genesis and evolution of association among human beings, of States and the social forms of humanity."[42]

And this is why Germany, which has been the most fruitful field for the development of the Darwinian theories, is also the most fruitful field for the intelligent, systematic propaganda of socialist ideas.

And it is precisely for this reason that in Berlin, in the windows of the book-stores of the socialist propaganda, the works of Charles Darwin occupy the place of honor beside those of Karl Marx.[43]

FOOTNOTES:

[37] LARFARGUE, *Le Matérialisme économique*, in *Ere nouvelle*, 1893.

[38] Avoiding both of the mutually exclusive theses that civilization is a consequence of race or a product of the environment, I have always maintained—by my theory of the natural factors in criminality—that it is the resultant of the combined action of the race and the environment.

Among the recent works which support the thesis of the exclusive or predominant influence of race, I must mention LE BON, *Les lois psychologiques de l'évolution des peuples*, Paris, 1894. This work is, however, very superficial. I refer the reader for a more thorough examination of these two theses to Chap. IV of my book *Omicidio nell' anthropologia criminale*, Turin, 1894.

[39] I use the expression "mercantile ethics," which LETOURNEAU used in his book on the Evolution of Ethics (*L'évolution de la morale*), Paris, 1887. In his scientific study of the facts relating to ethics, Letourneau has distinguished four phases: *animal* ethics—*savage* ethics—*barbarous* ethics—*mercantile* (or bourgeois) ethics; these phases will be followed by a higher phase of ethics which Malon has called *social* ethics.

[40] Some persons, still imbued with political (Jacobin) artificiality, think that in order to solve the social question it will be necessary to generalize the system of *métayage*. They imagine, then—though they do not say so—a royal or presidential decree: "Art. 1. Let all men become métayers!"

And it does not occur to them that if métayage, which was the rule, has become a less and less frequent exception, this must be the necessary result of natural causes.

The cause of the transformation is to be found in the fact that *métayage* represents (is a form typical of) petty agricultural industry, and that it is unable to compete with modern agricultural industry organized on a large scale and well equipped with machinery, just as handicrafts have not been able to endure competition with modern manufacturing industry. It is true that there still are to-day some handicraft industries in a few villages, but these are rudimentary organs which merely represent an anterior phase (of production), and which no longer have any important function in the economic world. They are, like the rudimentary organs of the higher species of animals, according to the theory of Darwin, permanent witnesses of past epochs.

The same Darwinian and economic law applies to *métayage*, which is also evidently destined to the same fate as handicrafts.

Conf. the excellent propagandist pamphlet of BIEL, *Ai contadini toscani*, Colle d' Elsa, 1894.

[41] HENRY GEORGE, Progress and Poverty, New York, 1898. Doubleday & McClure Co.

[42] L. JACOBY, *L'Idea dell' evoluzione*, in *Bibliotheca dell' economista*, série III, vol. IX, 2d part, p. 69.

[43] At the death of Darwin the *Sozialdemokrat* of the 27th of April, 1882, wrote: "The proletariat who are struggling for their emancipation will ever honor the memory of Charles Darwin."

Conf. LAFARGUE, *La théorie darwinienne*.

I am well aware that in these last years, perhaps in consequence of the relations between Darwinism and socialism, consideration has again been given to the objections to the theory of Darwin, made by Voegeli, and more recently by Weismann, on the hereditary transmissibility of acquired characters. See SPENCER, *The Inadequacy of Natural Selection*, Paris, 1894.— VIRCHOW, *Transformisme et descendance*, Berlin, 1893. But all this merely concerns such or such a detail of Darwinism, while the fundamental theory of metamorphic organic development remains impregnable.

PART SECOND.

EVOLUTION AND SOCIALISM.

The theory of universal evolution which—apart from such or such a more or less disputable detail—is truly characteristic of the vital tendency of modern scientific thought, has also been made to appear in absolute contradiction with the theories and the practical ideals of socialism.

In this case the fallacy is obvious.

If socialism is understood as that vague complex of sentimental aspirations so often crystallized into the artificial utopian creations of a new human world to be substituted by some sort of magic in a single day for the old world in which we live; then it is quite true that the scientific theory of evolution condemns the presumptions and the illusions of artificial or utopian political theories, which, whether they are reactionary or revolutionary, are always romantic, or in the words of the American Senator Ingalls, are "iridescent dreams."

But, unfortunately for our adversaries, contemporary socialism is an entirely different thing from the socialism which preceded the work of Marx. Apart from the same sentiment of protest against present injustices and the same aspirations toward a better future, there is nothing in common between these two socialisms, neither in their logical structure nor in their deductions, unless it be the clear vision, which in modern socialism becomes a mathematically exact prediction (thanks to the theories of evolution) of the final social organization—based on the collective ownership of the land and the means of production.

These are the conclusions to which we are led by the evidence of the facts—facts verified by a scientific examination of the three principal contradictions which our opponents have sought to set up between socialism and scientific evolution.

From this point it is impossible not to see the direct causal connection between Marxian socialism and scientific evolution, since it must be recognized that the former is simply the logical consequence of the application of the evolutionary theory to the domain of economics.

IX.

THE ORTHODOX THESIS AND THE SOCIALIST THESIS IN THE LIGHT OF THE EVOLUTION THEORY.

What, in substance, is the message of socialism? That the present economic world can not be immutable and eternal, that it merely represents a transitory phase of social evolution and that an ulterior phase, a differently organized world, is destined to succeed it.

That this new organization must be collectivist or socialist—and no longer individualist—results, as an ultimate and certain conclusion, from the examination we have made of Darwinism and socialism.

I must now demonstrate that this fundamental affirmation of socialism— leaving out of consideration for the moment all the details of that future organization, of which I will speak further on—is in perfect harmony with the experiential theory of evolutionism.

Upon what point are orthodox political economy and socialism in absolute conflict? Political economy has held and holds that the economic laws governing the production and distribution of wealth which it has established are *natural laws* ... not in the sense that they are laws naturally determined by the conditions of the social organism (which would be correct), but that they are *absolute laws*, that is to say that they apply to humanity at all times and in all places, and, consequently, that they are immutable in their principal points, though they may be subject to modification in details.[44]

Scientific socialism holds, on the contrary, that the laws established by classical political economy, since the time of Adam Smith, are laws peculiar to the present period in the history of civilized humanity, and that they are, consequently, laws essentially *relative* to the period of their analysis and discovery, and that just as they no longer fit the facts when the attempt is made to extend their application to past historical epochs and, still more, to pre-historic and ante-historic times, so it is absurd to attempt to apply them to the future and thus vainly try to petrify and perpetuate present social forms.

Of these two fundamental theses, the orthodox thesis and the socialist thesis, which is the one which best agrees with the scientific theory of universal evolution?

The answer can not be doubtful.[45]

The theory of evolution, of which Herbert Spencer was the true creator, by applying to sociology the tendency to relativism which the historical school had followed in its studies in law and political economy (even then heterodox on more than one point), has shown that everything changes; that the present phase—of the facts in astronomy, geology, biology and sociology—is only the resultant of thousands on thousands of incessant, inevitable, natural transformations; that the present differs from the past and that the future will certainly be different from the present.

Spencerism has done nothing but to collate a vast amount of scientific evidence, from all branches of human knowledge, in support of these two abstract thoughts of Leibnitz and Hegel: "The present is the child of the past, but it is the parent of the future," and "Nothing is; everything is becoming." This demonstration had already been made in the case of geology by Lyell who substituted for the traditional catastrophic theory of cataclysmic changes, the scientific theory of the gradual and continuous transformation of the earth.[46]

It is true that, notwithstanding his encyclopædic knowledge, Herbert Spencer has not made a really profound study of political economy, or that at least he has not furnished us the evidence of the *facts* to support his assertions in this field as he has done in the natural sciences. This does not alter the fact, however, that socialism is, after all, in its fundamental conception only the logical application of the scientific theory of natural evolution to economic phenomena.

It was Karl Marx who, in 1859 in his *Critique de l'économie politique*, and even before then, in 1847, in the famous *Manifesto* written in collaboration with Engels, nearly ten years before Spencer's *First Principles*, and finally in *Capital* (1867) supplemented, or rather completed, in the social domain, the scientific revolution begun by Darwin and Spencer.

The old metaphysics conceived of ethics—law—economics—as a finished compilation of absolute and eternal laws. This is the conception of Plato. It takes into consideration only historical times and it has, as an instrument of research, only the fantastic logic of the school-men. The generations which preceded us, have all been imbued with this notion of the absoluteness of natural laws, the conflicting laws of a dual universe of matter and spirit. Modern science, on the contrary, starts from the magnificent synthetic conception of monism, that is to say, of a single substance underlying all phenomena—matter and force being recognized as inseparable and indestructible, continuously evolving in a succession of forms—forms relative to their respective times and places. It has radically changed the direction of modern thought and directed it toward the grand idea of universal evolution.[47]

Ethics, law and politics are mere superstructures, effects of the economic structure; they vary with its variations, from one parallel (of latitude or longitude) to another, and from one century to another.

This is the great discovery which the genius of Karl Marx has expounded in his *Critique de l'économie politique*. I will examine further on the question as to what this sole source or basis of the varying economic conditions is, but the important point now is to emphasize their constant variability, from the pre-historic ages down to historical times and to the different periods of the latter.

Moral codes, religious creeds, juridical institutions both civil and criminal, political organization:—all are constantly undergoing transformation and all are relative to their respective historical and material environments.

To slay one's parents is the greatest of crimes in Europe and America; it is, on the contrary, a duty enjoined by religion in the island of Sumatra; in the same way, cannibalism is a permitted usage in Central Africa, and such it also was in Europe and America in pre-historic ages.

The family is, at first (as among animals), only a sort of sexual communism; then polyandry and the matriarchal system were established where the supply of food was scanty and permitted only a very limited increase of population; we find polygamy and the patriarchal system appearing whenever and wherever the tyranny of this fundamental economic cause of polyandry ceases to be felt; with the advent of historical times appears the monogamic form of the family the best and the most advanced form, although it is still requisite for it to be freed from the rigid conventionalism of the indissoluble tie and the disguised and legalised prostitution (the fruits of economic causes) which pollute it among us to-day.

How can any one hold that the constitution of property is bound to remain eternally just as it is, immutable, in the midst of the tremendous stream of changing social institutions and moral codes, all passing through evolutions and continuous and profound transformations? Property alone is subject to no changes and will remain petrified in its present form, *i. e.*, a monopoly by a few of the land and the means of production![48]

This is the absurd contention of economic and juridical orthodoxy. To the irresistible proofs and demonstrations of the evolutionist theory, they make only this one concession: the subordinate rules may vary, the *abuses* may be diminished. The principle itself is unassailable and a few individuals may seize upon and appropriate the land and the means of production necessary to the life of the whole social organism which thus remains completely and eternally under the more or less direct domination of those who have control over the physical foundation of life.[49]

Nothing more than a perfectly clear statement of the two fundamental theses—the thesis of classical law and economics, and the economic and juridical thesis of socialism—is necessary to determine, without further discussion, this first point of the controversy. At all events, the theory of evolution is in perfect, unquestionable harmony with the inductions of socialism and, or the contrary, it flatly contradicts the hypothesis of the absoluteness and immutability of the "natural" laws of economies, etc.

FOOTNOTES:

[44] U. RABBENO, *Le leggi economiche e il socialismo*, in *Rivista di filos. scientif.*, 1884, vol. III., fasc. 5.

[45] This is the thesis of COLAJANNI, in *Il socialismo*, Catane, 1884, P. 277. He errs when he thinks that I combatted this position in my book *Socialismo e criminalità*.

[46] MORSELLI, *Antropologia generale—Lezioni sull' uomo secondo la teoria dell' evoluzione*, Turin, 1890-94, gives an excellent *resumé* of these general indications of modern scientific thought in their application to all branches of knowledge from geology to anthropology.

[47] BONARDI, *Evoluzionismo e socialismo*, Florence, 1894.

[48] ARCANGELI, *Le evoluzioni della proprietà*, in *Critica sociale*, July 1, 1894.

[49] This is exactly analogous to the conflict between the partisans and the opponents of free-will.

The old metaphysics accorded to man (alone, a marvelous exception from all the rest of the universe) an absolutely free will.

Modern physio-psychology absolutely denies every form of the free-will dogma in the name of the laws of natural causality.

An intermediate position is occupied by those who, while recognizing that the freedom of man's will is not absolute, hold that at least a remnant of freedom must be conceded to the human will, because otherwise there would no longer be any merit or any blameworthiness, any vice or any virtue, etc.

I considered this question in my first work: *Teoria dell' imputabilità e negazione del libero arbitrio* (Florence, 1878, out of print), and in the third chapter of my *Sociologie criminelle*, French trans., Paris, 1892.

I speak of it here only in order to show the analogy in the form of the debate on the economico-social question, and therefore the possibility of predicting a similar ultimate solution.

The true conservative, drawing his inspiration from the metaphysical tradition, sticks to the old philosophical or economic ideas with all their rigid absolutism; at least he is logical.

The determinist, in the name of science, upholds diametrically opposite ideas, in the domain of psychology as well as in those of the economic or juridical sciences.

The eclectic, in politics as in psychology, in political economy as in law, is a conservative through and through, but he fondly hopes to escape the difficulties of the conservative position by making a few partial concessions to save appearances. But if the eclecticism is a convenient and agreeable attitude for its champions, it is, like hybridism, sterile, and neither life nor science owe anything to it.

Therefore, the socialists are logical when they contend that in the last analysis there are only two political parties: the individualists (conservatives [or Republicans], progressives [or Democrats] and radicals [or Populists]) and the socialists.

X.

THE LAW OF APPARENT RETROGRESSION AND COLLECTIVE OWNERSHIP.

Admitting, say our adversaries, that in demanding a social transformation socialism is in apparent accord with the evolutionist theory, it does not follow that its positive conclusions—notably the substitution of social ownership for individual ownership—are justified by that theory. Still further, they add, we maintain that those conclusions are in absolute contradiction with that very theory, and that they are therefore, to say the least, utopian and absurd.

The first alleged contradiction between socialism and evolutionism is that the return to collective ownership of the land would be, at the same time, a return to the primitive, savage state of mankind, and socialism would indeed be a transformation, but a transformation in a backward direction, that is to say, against the current of the social evolution which has led us from the primitive form of collective property in land to the present form of individual property in land—the form characteristic of advanced civilization. Socialism, then, would be a return to barbarism.

This objection contains an element of truth which can not be denied; it rightly points out that collective ownership should be a return—apparent— to the primitive social organization. But the conclusion drawn from this truth is absolutely false and anti-scientific because it altogether neglects a law—which is usually forgotten—but which is no less true, no less founded on scientific observation of the facts than is the law of social evolution.

This is a sociological law which an able French physician merely pointed out in his studies on the relations between Transmutation and Socialism,[50] and the truth and full importance of which I showed in my *Sociologie criminelle* (1892)—before I became a militant socialist—and which I again emphasized in my recent controversy with Morselli on the subject of divorce.[51]

This law of apparent retrogression proves that the reversion of social institutions to primitive forms and types is a fact of constant recurrence.

Before referring to some obvious illustrations of this law, I would recall to your notice the fact that M. Cognetti de Martiis, as far back as 1881, had a vague perception of this sociological law. His work, *Forme primitive nell' evoluzione economica*, (Turin, 1881), so remarkable for the fullness, accuracy and reliability of its collation of relevant facts, made it possible to foresee the possibility of the reappearance in the future economic evolution of the primitive forms characteristic of the status which formed the starting-point of the social evolution.

I also remember having heard Carducci say, in his lectures at the University of Bologna, that the later development of the forms and the substance of literature is often merely the reproduction of the forms and the substance of the primitive Græco-Oriental literature; in the same way, the modern scientific theory of monism, the very soul of universal evolution and the typical and definitive form of systematic, scientific, experiential human thought boldly fronting the facts of the external world—following upon the brilliant but erratic speculations of metaphysics—is only a return to the ideas of the Greek philosophers and of Lucretius, the great poet of naturalism.

The examples of this reversion to primitive forms are only too obvious and too numerous, even in the category of social institutions.

I have already spoken of the religions evolution. According to Hartmann, in the primitive stage of human development happiness appeared attainable during the lifetime of the individual; this appeared impossible later on and its realization was referred to the life beyond the tomb; and now the tendency is to refer its realization to the earthly life of humanity, not to the life of the individual as in primitive times, but to series of generations yet unborn.

The same is true in the political domain. Herbert Spencer remarks (Principles of Sociology, Vol. II, Part V, Chap. V,) that the will of all—the sovereign element among primitive mankind—gradually gives way to the will of a single person, then to those of a few (these are the various aristocracies: military, hereditary, professional or feudal), and the popular will finally tends again to become sovereign with the progress of democracy (universal suffrage—the referendum—direct legislation by the people, etc.).

The right to administer punishment, a simple defensive function among primitive mankind tends to become the same once more. Criminal law no longer pretends to be a teleological agency for the distribution of ideal justice. This pretension in former days was an illusion that the belief in the freedom of the will had erected on the natural foundation of society's right of self-defense. Scientific investigations into the nature of crime, as a natural and social phenomenon, have demonstrated to-day how absurd and unjustified was the pretension of the lawmaker and the judge to weigh and measure the guilt of the delinquent to make the punishment exactly counterbalance it, instead of contenting themselves with excluding from civil society, temporarily or permanently, the individuals unable to adapt themselves to its requirements, as is done in the case of the insane and the victims of contagious diseases.

The same truth applies to marriage. The right of freely dissolving the tie, which was recognized in primitive society, has been gradually replaced by the absolute formulæ of theology and mysticism which fancy that the "free will" can settle the destiny of a person by a monosyllable pronounced at a time when the physical equilibrium is as unstable as it is during courtship and at marriage. Later on the reversion to the spontaneous and primitive form of a union based on mutual consent imposes itself on men, and the matrimonial union, with the increase in the frequency and facility of divorce, reverts to its original forms and restores to the family, that it to say to the social cell, a healthier constitution.

This some phenomenon may be traced in the organization of property. Spencer himself has been forced to recognize that there has been an inexorable tendency to a reversion to primitive collectivism since ownership in land, at first a family attribute, then industrial, as he has himself demonstrated, has reached its culminating point, so that in some countries (Torrens act in Australia) land has become a sort of *personal* property, transferable as readily as a share in a stock-company.

Read as proof what such an *individualist* as Herbert Spencer has written:

"At first sight it seems fairly inferable that the absolute ownership of land by private persons, must be the *ultimate* state which industrialism brings about. But though industrialism has thus far tended to individualize possession of land, while individualizing all other possession, *it may be doubted whether the final stage is at present reached*. Ownership established by force does not stand on the same footing as ownership established by contract, and though multiplied sales and purchases, treating the two ownerships in the same way, have tacitly assimilated them, the assimilation may eventually be denied. The analogy furnished by assumed rights of possession over human beings, helps us to recognize this possibility. For while prisoners of war, taken by force and held as property in a vague way (being at first much on a footing with other members of a household), were reduced more definitely to the form of property when the buying and selling of slaves became general; and while it might, centuries ago, have been thence inferred that the ownership of man by man was an ownership in course of being permanently established;[52] yet we see that a later stage of civilization, reversing this process, has destroyed ownership of man by man. Similarly, at a stage still more advanced, it may be that *private ownership of land will disappear*."[53]

Moreover, this process of the socialization of property, though a partial and subordinate process, is nevertheless so evident and continuous that to deny its existence would be to maintain that the economic and consequently the juridical tendency of the organization of property is not in the direction of a greater and greater magnification of the interests and rights of the collectivity over those of the individual. This, which is only a preponderance to-day, will become by an inevitable evolution a complete substitution as regards property in land and the means of production.

The fundamental thesis of Socialism is then, to repeat it again, in perfect harmony with that sociological law of apparent retrogression, the natural reasons for which have been so admirably analyzed by M. Loria, thus: the thought and the life of primitive mankind are moulded and directed by the natural environment along the simplest and most fundamental lines; then the progress of intelligence and the complexity of life increasing by a law of evolution give us an analytical development of the principal elements contained in the first genus of each institution; this analytical development is often, when once finished, detrimental to each one of its elements; humanity itself, arrived at a certain stage of evolution, reconstructs and combines in a final synthesis these different elements, and thus returns to its primitive starting-point.[54]

This reversion to primitive forms is not, however, a pure and simple repetition. Therefore it is called the law of *apparent* retrogression, and this removes all force from the objection that socialism would be a "return to primitive *barbarism*." It is not a pure and simple repetition, but it is the concluding phase of a cycle, of a grand rhythm, as M. Asturaro recently put it, which infallibly and inevitably preserves in their integrity the achievements and conquests of the long preceding evolution, in so far as they are vital and fruitful; and the final outcome is far superior, objectively and subjectively, to the primitive social embryo.

The track of the social evolution is not represented by a closed circle, which, like the serpent in the old symbol, cuts off all hope of a better future; but, to use the figure of Goethe, it is represented by a spiral, which seems to return upon itself, but which always advances and ascends.

FOOTNOTES:

[50] L. DRAMARD, *Transformisme et socialisme*, in *Revue Socialiste*, Jan. and Feb., 1885.

[51] *Divorzio e sociologia*, in *Scuola positiva nella geurisprudenza penale*, Rome, 1893, No. 16.

[52] It is known that Aristotle, mistaking for an absolute sociological law a law relative to his own time, declared that slavery was a natural institution,

and that men were divided, *by Nature*, into two classes—free men and slaves.

[53] SPENCER, Principles of Sociology, Vol. II, Part. V., Chap. XV., p. 553. New York, 1897. D. Appleton & Co.

This idea, which Spencer had expressed in 1850 in his *Social Statics* is found again in his recent work, *Justice* (Chap. XI, and Appendix 3). It is true that he has made a step backward. He thinks that the amount of the indemnity to be given to the present holders of the land would be so great that this would make next to impossible that "nationalization of the land" which, as long ago as 1881, Henry George considered as the only *remedy*, and that Gladstone had the courage to propose as a solution of the Irish question. Spencer adds: "I adhere to the inference originally drawn, *that the aggregate of men forming the community are the supreme owners of the land*, but a fuller consideration of the matter has led me to the conclusion that individual ownership, subject to State suzerainty, should be maintained."

The "profound study" which Spencer has made in Justice—(and, let us say between parentheses, this work, together with his "*Positive and Negative Beneficence*" furnishes sad evidence of the senile mental retrogression that even Herbert Spencer has been unable to escape; moreover its subjective aridity is in strange contrast with the marvelous wealth of scientific evidence poured forth in his earlier works)—is based on these two arguments: I. The present landed proprietors are not the direct descendants of the first conquerors; they have, in general, acquired their titles by free contract; II. Society is entitled to the ownership of the virgin soil, as it was before it was cleared, before any improvements or buildings were put upon it by private owners; the indemnity which would have to be paid for these improvements would reach an enormous figure.

The answer is that the first argument would hold good if socialism proposed to *punish* the present owners; but the question presents itself in a different form. Society places the expropriation of the owners of land on the ground of "public utility," and the individual right must give way before the rights of society. Just as it does at present, leaving out of consideration for the moment the question of indemnity. To reply to the second argument, in the first place, it must not be forgotten that the improvements are not exclusively the work of the personal exertions of the owners. They represent, at first, an enormous accumulation of fatigue and blood that many generations of laborers have left upon the soil, in order to bring it to its present state of cultivation ... and all of this for the profit of others; there is also this fact to be remembered that society itself, the social life, has been a great factor in producing these improvements (or increased values), since public roads, railways, the use of machinery in agriculture, etc., have been the means of bestowing freely upon the landowners large unearned increments that have greatly swollen the prices of their lands.

Why, finally, if we are to consider the amount and the character of this indemnity, should this indemnity be *total* and *absolute*? Why, even under present conditions, if a landowner, for various reasons, such as cherished memories connected with the land, values it at a sentimental price, he would be forced under the right of eminent domain to accept the market value, without any extra payment for his affection or sentiment. It would be just the same in the case of the collective appropriation which would, moreover, be facilitated by the progressive concentration of the land in the hands of a few great landed proprietors. If we were to assure these proprietors, *for the term of the natural lives*, a comfortable and tranquil life, it would suffice to make the indemnity meet all the requirements of the most rigorous equity.

[54] LORIA, *La Teoria economica della constituzione politica*, Turin, 1886. p. 141. The second edition of this work has appeared in French, considerably enlarged: *Les bases économiques de la constitution sociale*, Paris, 1893. (This has also been translated into English.—Tr.)

This law of apparent retrogression alone overthrows the greater part of the far too superficial criticisms that Guyot makes upon socialism in *La Tyrannie socialiste*, Paris, 1893 (published in English, by Swan Sonnenschein, London,) and in *Les Principes de 1789 et le Socialisme*, Paris, 1894.

XI.

THE SOCIAL EVOLUTION AND INDIVIDUAL LIBERTY.

The conclusion of the preceding chapter will be of use to us in the examination of the second contradiction that, it is pretended, exists between socialism and the theory of evolution. It is asserted and repeated in all possible tones that socialism constitutes a tyranny under a new form which will destroy all the blessings of liberty won with such toil and difficulty in our century, at the cost of so many sacrifices and of so many martyrs.

I have already shown, in speaking of anthropological inequalities, that socialism will, on the contrary, assure to all individuals the conditions of a human existence and the possibility of developing with the utmost freedom and completeness their own respective individualities.

It is sufficient here for me to refer to another law, which the scientific theory of evolution has established, to demonstrate (since I cannot in this monograph enter into details) that it is an error to assume that the advent of socialism would result in the suppression of the vital and vitalizing part of personal and political liberty.

It is a law of natural evolution, set forth and illustrated with remarkable clearness by M. Ardigò[55], that each succeeding phase of the natural and social evolution does not destroy the vital and life-giving manifestations of the preceding phases, but that, on the contrary, it preserves their existence in so far as they are vital and only eliminates their pathological manifestations.

In the biological evolution, the manifestations of vegetable life do not efface the first glimmerings of the dawn of life that are seen even before in the crystallization of minerals, any more than the manifestations of animal life efface those of vegetable life. The human form of life also permits the continued existence of the forms and links which precede it in the great series of living beings, but, more than this, the later forms only really live in so far as they are the product of the primitive forms and co-exist with them.

The social evolution follows the same law: and this is precisely the interpretation of transition periods given by scientific evolutionism. They did not annihilate the conquests of the preceding civilizations, but they preserved, on the contrary, whatever was vital in them and fecundated them for the Renaissance of a new civilization.

This law, which dominates all the magnificent development of the social life, equally governs the fate and the parabolic career of all social institutions.

One phase of social evolution by following upon another phase eliminates, it is true, the parts that are not vital, the pathological products of preceding institutions, but it preserves and develops the parts that are healthy and vigorous while ever elevating more and more the physical and moral diapason of humanity.

By this natural process the great stream of humanity issued from the virgin forests of savage life and developed with majestic grandeur during the periods of barbarism and the present civilization, which are superior in some respects to the preceding phases of the social life, but in many others are marred by the very products of their own degeneracy, as I pointed out in speaking of reactionary varieties of social selection.

And, as an example of this, it is certain that the laborers of the contemporaneous period, of the bourgeois civilization have, in general, a better physical and moral life than those of past centuries, but it cannot be denied none the less that their condition as free *wage-workers* is inferior in more than one particular to the condition of the *slaves* of antiquity and of the *serfs* of the Middle Ages.

The *slave* of antiquity was, it is true, the absolute property of his master, of the *free* man, and he was condemned to well nigh an animal existence, but it was to the interest of his master to assure him daily bread at the least, for the slave formed a part of his estate, like his cattle and horses.

Just so, the serf or villein of the Middle Ages enjoyed certain customary rights which attached him to the soil and assured him at the least—save in case of famine—of daily bread.

The free wage-worker of the modern world, on the contrary, is always condemned to labor inhuman both in its duration and its character, and this is the justification of that demand for an Eight-Hours day which can already count more than one victory and which is destined to a sure triumph. As no permanent legal relation binds the wage-slave either to the capitalist proprietor or to the soil, his daily bread is not assured to him, because the proprietor no longer has any interest to feed and support the laborers who toil in his factory or on his field. The death or sickness of the laborer cannot, in fact, cause any decrease of his estate and he can always draw from the inexhaustible multitude of laborers who are forced by lack of employment to offer themselves on the market.

That is why—not because present-day proprietors are more wicked than those of former times, but because even the moral sentiments are the result of economic conditions—the landed proprietor or the superintendent of his estate hastens to have a veterinary called if, in his stable, a cow becomes ill, while he is in no hurry to have a doctor called if it is the son of the cow-herd who is attacked by disease.

Certainly there may be—and these are more or less frequent exceptions—here and there a proprietor who contradicts this rule, especially when he lives in daily contact with his laborers. Neither can it be denied that the rich classes are moved at times by the spirit of benevolence—even apart from the *charity fad*—and that they thus put to rest the inner voice, the symptom of the moral disease from which they suffer, but the inexorable rule is nevertheless as follows: with the modern form of industry the laborer has gained political liberty, the right of suffrage, of association, etc. (rights which he is allowed to use only when he does not utilize them to form a class-party, based on intelligent apprehension of the essential point of the social question), but he has lost the guarantee of daily bread and of a home.

Socialism wishes to give this guarantee to all individuals—and it demonstrates the mathematical possibility of this by the substitution of social ownership for individual ownership of the means of production—but it does not follow from this that socialism will do away with all the useful and truly fruitful conquests of the present phase of civilization, and of the preceding phases.

And here is a characteristic example of this: the invention of industrial and agricultural machinery, that marvelous application of science to the transformation of natural forces which ought to have had only beneficent consequences, has caused and is still causing the misery and ruin of thousands and thousands of laborers. The substitution of machines for human labor has inevitably condemned multitudes of workers to the tortures of enforced idleness and to the ruthless action of the iron law of minimum wages barely sufficient to prevent them from dying of hunger.

The first instinctive reaction or impulse of these unfortunates was and still is, unhappily, to destroy the machines and to see in them only the instruments of their undeserved sufferings.

But the destruction of the machines would be, in fact, only a pure and simple return to barbarism, and this is not the wish or purpose of socialism which represents a higher phase of human civilization.

And this is why socialism alone can furnish a solution of this tragic difficulty which can not be solved by economic individualism which involves the constant employment and introduction of improved machinery because its use gives an evident and irresistible advantage to the capitalist.

It is necessary—and there is no other solution—that the machines become collective or social property. Then, obviously, their only effect will be to diminish the aggregate amount of labor and muscular effort necessary to produce a given quantity of products. And thus the daily work of each worker will be decreased, and his standard of existence will constantly rise and become more closely correspondent with the dignity of a human being.

This effect is already manifest, to a limited extent, in those cases where, for instance, several small farm proprietors found co-operative societies for the purchase of, for example, threshing-machines. If there should be joined to the small proprietors, in a grand fraternal co-operation, the laborers or peasants (and this will be possible only when the land shall have become social property), and if the machines were municipal property, for example, as are the fire-engines, and if the commune were to grant their use for the labors of the fields, the machines would no longer produce any evil effects and all men would see in them their liberators.

It is thus that socialism, because it represents a higher phase of human evolution, would eliminate from the present phase only the bad products of our unbridled economic individualism which creates, at one pole, the billionaires or "Napoleons of Finance" who enrich themselves in a few years by seizing upon—in ways more or less clearly described in the penal code—the public funds, and which, at the other pole, accumulates vast multitudes of poverty-stricken wretches in the slums of the cities or in the houses of straw and mud which reproduce in the South of Italy, the quarters of the Helots of antiquity, or in the valley of the Po, the huts of the Australian bushmen.[56]

No intelligent socialist has ever dreamt of not recognizing all that the bourgeoisie has done for human civilization, or of tearing out the pages of gold that it has written in the history of the civilized world by its brilliant development of the various nations, by its marvelous applications of science to industry, and by the commercial and intellectual relations which it has developed between different peoples.

These are permanent conquests of human progress, and socialism does not deny them any more than it wishes to destroy them, and it accords a just tribute of recognition to the generous pioneers who have achieved them. The attitude of socialism toward the bourgeoisie might be compared to that of atheists who do not wish either to destroy or to refuse their admiration to a painting of Raphael or to a statue of Michel-Angelo, because these works represent and give the seal of eternity to religious legends.

But socialism sees in the present bourgeois civilization, arrived at its decline, the sad symptoms of an irremediable dissolution, and it contends that it is necessary to rid the social organism of its infectious *poison*, and this not by ridding it of such or such a bankrupt, of such or such a corrupt official, of such or such a dishonest contractor ... but by going to the root of the evil, to the indisputable source of the virulent infection. By radically transforming the regime—through the substitution of social ownership for individual ownership—it is necessary to renew the healthy and vital forces of human society, to enable it to rise to a higher phase of civilization. Then, it is true, the privileged classes will no longer be able to pass their lives in idleness, luxury and dissipation, and they will have to make up their minds to lead an industrious and less ostentatious life, but the immense majority of men will rise to the heights of serene dignity, security and joyous brotherhood, instead of living in the sorrows, anxieties and bitter strife of the present.

An analogous response may be made to that banal objection that socialism will suppress all liberty—that objection repeated to satiety by all those who more or less consciously conceal, under the colors of political liberalism, the tendencies of economic conservatism.

That repugnance which many people, even in good faith, show toward socialism, is it not the manifestation of another law of human evolution which Herbert Spencer has formulated thus: "Every progress effected is an obstacle to further progress"?

This is, in fact, a natural psychological tendency, a tendency analogous to *fetishism*, to refuse to consider the ideal attained, the progress effected as a simple instrument, a starting-point for further progress and for the attainment of new ideals, instead of contentedly halting to adore as a fetish the progress already effected, which men are prone to look upon as being so complete that it leaves no room for new ideals and higher aspirations.

Just as the savage adores the fruit-tree, whose benefits he enjoys, for itself and not for the fruits it can yield, and, in the end, makes a fetish of it, an idol too holy to be touched and, therefore, barren; just as the miser who has learned in our individualist world the value of money, ends by adoring the money in itself and for itself, as a fetish and an idol, and keeps it buried in a safe where it remains sterile, instead of employing it as a means for procuring himself new pleasures; in the same way, the sincere liberal, the son of the French Revolution, has made Liberty an idol which is its own goal, a sterile fetish, instead of making use of it as an instrument for new conquests, for the realization of new ideals.

It is understood that under a regime of political tyranny, the first and most urgent ideal was necessarily the conquest of liberty and of political sovereignty.

And we who arrive upon the field after the battle is fought and the victory won, we gladly pay our tribute of gratitude for that conquest to all the martyrs and heroes who bought it at the price of their blood.

But Liberty is not and can not be its own end and object!

What is the liberty of holding public assemblages or the liberty of thought worth if the stomach has not its daily bread, and if millions of individuals have their moral strength paralyzed as a consequence of bodily or cerebral anemia?

Of what worth is the theoretic share in political sovereignty, the right to vote, if the people remain enslaved by misery, lack of employment, and acute or chronic hunger?

Liberty for liberty's sake—there you have the progress achieved turned into an obstacle to future progress; it is a sort of political masturbation, it is impotency face to face with the new necessities of life.

Socialism, on the other hand, says that just as the subsequent phase of the social evolution does not efface the conquests of the preceding phases, neither does it wish to suppress the liberty so gloriously conquered, by the bourgeois world in 1789—but it does desire the laborers, after they have become conscious of the interests and needs of their class, to make use of that liberty to realize a more equitable and more human social organization.

Nevertheless, it is only too indisputable that under the system of private property and its inevitable consequence, the monopoly of economic power, the liberty of the man who does not share in this monopoly, is only an impotent and sentimental toy. And when the workers, with a clear consciousness of their class-interests, wish to make use of this liberty, then the holders of political power are forced to disown the great liberal principles, "the principles of '89," by suppressing all public liberty, and they vainly fancy that they will be able, in this way, to stop the inevitable march of human evolution.

As much must be said of another accusation made against socialists. They renounce their fatherland (*patrie*), it is said, in the name of internationalism.

This also is false.

The national *épopées* which, in our century, have reconquered for Italy and Germany their unity and their independence, have really constituted great steps forward, and we are grateful to those who have given us a free country.

But our country can not become an obstacle to future progress, to the fraternity of all peoples, freed from national hatreds which are truly a relic of barbarism, or a mere bit of theatrical scenery to hide the interests of capitalism which has been shrewd enough to realize, for its own benefit, the broadest internationalism.

It was a true moral and social progress to rise above the phase of the communal wars in Italy, and to feel ourselves all brothers of one and the same nation; it will be just the same when we shall have risen above the phase of "patriotic" rivalries to feel ourselves all brothers of one and the same humanity.

It is, nevertheless, not difficult for us to penetrate, thanks to the historical key of class-interests, the secret of the contradictions, in which the classes in power move. When they form an international league—the London banker, thanks to telegraphy, is master of the markets in Pekin, New York and St. Petersburg—it is greatly to the advantage of that ruling class to maintain the artificial divisions between the laborers of the whole world, or even those of old Europe alone, because it is only the division of the workers which makes possible the maintenance of the power of the capitalists. And to attain their object, it suffices to exploit the primitive fund of savage hatred for "foreigners."

But this does not keep international socialism from being, even from this point of view, a definite moral scheme and an inevitable phase of human evolution.

Just so, and in consequence of the same sociological law, it is not correct to assert that, by establishing collective ownership, socialism will suppress every kind of individual ownership.

We must repeat again that one phase of evolution can not suppress all that has been accomplished during the preceding phases; it suppresses only the manifestations which have ceased to be vital, and it suppresses them because they are in contradiction with the new conditions of existence begotten by the new phases of evolution.

In substituting social ownership for individual ownership of the land and the means of production, it is obvious that it will not be necessary to suppress private property in the food necessary to the individual, nor in clothing and objects of personal use which will continue to be objects of individual or family consumption.

This form of individual ownership will then always continue to exist, since it is necessary and perfectly consistent with social ownership of the land, mines, factories, houses, machines, tools and instruments of labor, and means of transportation.

The collective ownership of libraries—which we see in operation under our eyes—does it deprive individuals of the personal use of rare and expensive books which they would be unable to procure in any other way, and does it not largely increase the utility that can be derived from these books, when compared to the services that these books could render if they were shut up in the private library of a useless book-collector? In the same way, the collective ownership of the land and the means of production, by securing to everyone the use of the machines, tools and land, will only increase their utility a hundred-fold.

And let no one say that, when men shall no longer have the exclusive and transferable (by inheritance, etc.) *ownership* of wealth, they will no longer be impelled to labor because they will no longer be constrained to work by personal or family self-interest.[57] We see, for example, that, even in our present individualist world, those survivals of collective property in land— to which Laveleye has so strikingly called the attention of sociologists— continue to be cultivated and yield a return which is not lower than that yielded by lands held in private ownership, although these communist or collectivist farmers have only the right of use and enjoyment, and not the absolute title.[58]

If some of these survivals of collective ownership are disappearing, or if their administration is bad, this can not be an argument against socialism, since it is easy to understand that, in the present economic organization based on absolute individualism, these organisms do not have an environment which furnishes them the conditions of a possible existence.

It is as though one were to wish a fish to live out of water, or a mammal in an atmosphere containing no oxygen.

These are the same considerations which condemn to a certain death all those famous experiments—the socialist, communist or anarchist colonies which it has been attempted to establish in various places as "experimental trials of socialism." It seems not to have been understood that such experiments could only result in inevitable abortions, obliged as they are to develop in an individualist economic and moral environment which can not furnish them the conditions essential for their physiological development, conditions which they will, on the contrary, have when the whole social organization shall be guided by the collectivist principle, that is to say, when society shall be *socialized*.[59]

Then individual tendencies and psychological aptitudes will adapt themselves to the environment. It is natural that in an individualist environment, a world of free competition, in which every individual sees in every other if not an adversary, at least a competitor, anti-social egoism should be the tendency which is inevitably most highly developed, as a necessary result of the instinct of self-preservation, especially in these latest phases of a civilization which seems to be driven at full steam, compared to the pacific and gentle individualism of past centuries.

In an environment where every one, in exchange for intellectual or manual labor furnished to society, will be assured of his daily bread and will thus be saved from daily anxiety, it is evident that egoism will have far fewer stimulants, fewer occasions to manifest itself than solidarity, sympathy and altruism will have. Then that pitiless maxim—*homo homini lupus*—will cease to be true—a maxim which, whether we admit it or not, poisons so much of our present life.

I can not dwell longer on these details and I conclude here the examination of this second pretended opposition between socialism and evolution by again pointing out that the sociological law which declares that the subsequent phase (of social evolution) does not efface the vital and fruitful manifestations of the preceding phases of evolution, gives us, in regard to the social organization in process of formation, a more exact (*positive* or fact-founded) idea than our opponents think, who always imagine that they have to refute the romantic and sentimental socialism of the first half of this century.[60]

This shows how little weight there is in the objection recently raised against socialism, in the name of a learned but vague sociological eclecticism, by a distinguished Italian professor, M. Vanni.

"Contemporary socialism is not identified with individualism, since it places at the foundation of the social organization a principle which is not that of individual autonomy, but rather its negation. If, notwithstanding this, it promulgates individualist ideas, which are in contradiction with its principles, this does not signify that it has changed its nature, or that it has ceased to be socialism: it means simply that it lives upon and by contradictions."[61]

When socialism, by assuring to every one the means of livelihood, contends that it will permit the assertion and the development of all individualities, it does not fall into a contradiction of principles, but being, as it is, the approaching phase of human civilization, it can not suppress nor efface whatever is vital, that is to say, compatible with the new social form, in the preceding phases. And just as socialist internationalism is not in conflict with patriotism, since it recognizes whatever is healthy and true in that sentiment, and eliminates only the pathological part, jingoism, in the same way, socialism does not draw its life from contradiction, but it follows, on the contrary, the fundamental laws of natural evolution, in developing and preserving the vital part of individualism, and in suppressing only its pathological manifestations which are responsible for the fact that in the modern world, as Prampolini said, 90 per cent. of the cells of the social organization are condemned to anemia because 10 per cent. are ill with hyper-emia and hyper-trophy.

FOOTNOTES:

[55] ARDIGÒ, *La formazione naturale*, Vol. II. of his *Opere filosofiche*, Padua, 1897.

[56] My master, Pietro Ellero, has given in *La Tirrandie borghese*, an eloquent description of this social and political pathology as it appears in Italy.

[57] RICHTER, *Où mène le socialisme*, Paris, 1892.

[58] M. Loria, in *Les Bases économiques de la constitution sociale*, Paris, 1894, part 1st, demonstrates, moreover, that in a society based on collective ownership selfishness, rightly understood will still remain the principal motive of human actions, but that it will then be the means of realizing a social harmony of which it is the worst enemy under the regime of individualism.

Here is an example of this, on a small scale, but instructive. The means of transportation have, in large cities, followed the ordinary process of progressive socialization. At first, everybody went on foot, excepting only a few rich persons who were able to have horses and carriages; later, carriages were made available for the public at a fixed rate of hire (the *fiacres* which have been used in Paris a little more than a century, and which took their name from Saint Fiacre because the first cab stood beneath his image); then, the dearness of *fiacre*-hire led to a further socialization by means of omnibuses and tramways. Another step forward and the socialization will be complete. Let the cab service, omnibus service, street railways, *bicyclettes*, etc., become a municipal service or function and every one will be able to make use of it gratis just as he freely enjoys the railways when they become a national public service.

But, then—this is the individualist objection—everybody will wish to ride in cabs or on trolleys, and the service having to attempt to satisfy all, will be perfectly satisfactory to no one.

This is not correct. If the transformation had to be made suddenly, this might be a temporary consequence. But even now many ride gratis (on passes, etc.) on both railways and tramways.

And so it seems to us that every one will wish to ride on the street cars because the fact that it is now impossible for many to enjoy this mode of locomotion gives rise to the desire for the forbidden fruit. But when the enjoyment of it shall be free (and there could be restrictions based on the necessity for such transportation) another egoistic motive will come into play—the physiological need of walking, especially for well-fed people who have been engaged in sedentary labor.

And so you see how individual selfishness, in this example of collective ownership on a small scale, would act in harmony with the social requirements.

[59] Thus it is easy to understand how unfounded is the reasoning among the opponents of socialism that the failure of communist or socialist colonies is an objective demonstration of "the instability of a socialist arrangement" (of society).

[60] This is what Yves Guyot, for example, does in *Les Principes de 1789*, Paris, 1894, when he declares, in the name of individualist psychology, that "socialism is restrictive and individualism expansive." This thesis is, moreover, in part true, if it is transposed.

The vulgar psychology, which answers the purposes of M. Guyot (*La Tyrannie socialiste*, liv. III, ch. I.), is content with superficial observations. It declares, for instance, that if the laborer works twelve hours, he will produce evidently a third more than if he works eight hours, and this is the reason why industrial capitalism has opposed and does oppose the minimum programme of the three eighths—eight hours for work, eight hours for sleep and eight hours for meals and recreation.

A more scientific physio-psychological observation demonstrates, on the contrary, as I said long ago, that "man is a machine, but he does not function after the fashion of a machine," in the sense that man is a living machine, and not an inorganic machine.

Every one knows that a locomotive or a sewing machine does in twelve hours a quantity of work greater by one-third than it does in eight hours; but man is a living machine, subject to the law of physical mechanics, but also to those of biological mechanics. Intellectual labor, like muscular labor, is not uniform in quality and intensity throughout its duration. Within the individual limits of *fatigue* and exhaustion, it obeys the law which Quetelet expressed by his binomial curve, and which I believe to be one of the fundamental laws of living and inorganic nature. At the start the force or the speed is very slight—afterward a maximum of force or speed is attained—and at last the force or speed again becomes very slight.

With manual labor, as with intellectual labor, there is a maximum, after which the muscular and cerebral forces decline, and then the work drags along slowly and without vigor until the end of the forced daily labor. Consider also the beneficient *suggestive* influence of a reduction of hours, and you will readily understand why the recent English reports are so unanswerable on the excellent results, even from the capitalist point of view, of the Eight-Hour reform. The workingmen are less fatigued, and the production is undiminished.

When these economic reforms, and all those which are based on an exact physio-psychology, shall be effected under the socialist regime—that is to say, without the friction and the loss of force that would be inevitable under capitalist individualism—it is evident that they will have immense material and moral advantages, notwithstanding the *a priori* objections of the present individualism which can not see or which forgets the profound reflex effects of a change of the social environment on individual psychology.

[61] ICILIO VANNI, *La funzione practica della filosofia del diritto considerata in sè e in rapporto al socialismo contemporaneo*, Bologne, 1894.

XII.

EVOLUTION—REVOLUTION—REBELLION— INDIVIDUAL VIOLENCE—SOCIALISM AND ANARCHY.

The last and the gravest of the contradictions that it is attempted to set up between socialism and the scientific theory of evolution, relates to the question of *how* socialism, in practice, will be inaugurated and realized.

Some think that socialism ought, at the present time, to set forth, in all its details, the precise and symmetrical form of the future social organization.—"Show me a practical description of the new society, and I will then decide whether I ought to prefer it to the present society."

Others—and this is a consequence of that first false conception—imagine that socialism wishes in a single day to change the face of the world, and that we will be able to go to sleep in a world completely bourgeois and to wake up next morning in a world completely socialist.

How is it possible not to see, some one then says, that all this is directly and thoroughly in conflict with the law of evolution, a law based on the two fundamental ideas—which are characteristic of the new tendencies of scientific thought and which are in conflict with the old metaphysics—of the *naturalness* and the *gradualness* of all phenomena in all domains of universal life, from astronomy to sociology.

It is indisputable that these two objections were, in great part, well founded when they were directed against what Engels has called "utopian socialism."

When socialism, before the time of Karl Marx, was merely the sentimental expression of a humanitarianism as noble as it was neglectful of the most elementary principles of exact science, it was altogether natural for its partisans to give rein to the impetuosity of their generous natures both in their vehement protests against social injustices and in their reveries and day-dreams of a better world, to which the imagination strove to give precise contours, as witness all the utopias from the REPUBLIC of Plato to the LOOKING BACKWARD of Bellamy.

It is easy to understand what opportunities these constructions afforded to criticism. The latter was false in part, moreover, because it was the offspring of the habits of thought peculiar to the modern world, and which will change with the change in the environment, but it was well founded in part also because the enormous complexity of social phenomena makes it impossible to prophesy in regard to all the details of a social organization which will differ from ours more profoundly than the present society differs from that of the Middle Ages, because the bourgeois world has retained the same foundation, individualism, as the society which preceded it, while the socialist world will have a fundamentally different polarization.

These prophetic constructions of a new social order are, moreover, the natural product of that artificiality in politics and sociology, with which the most orthodox individualists are equally deeply imbued, individualists who imagine, as Spencer has remarked, that human society is like a piece of dough to which the law can give one form rather than another, without taking into account the organic and psychical, ethical and historical qualities, tendencies and aptitudes of the different peoples.

Sentimental socialism has furnished some attempts at utopian construction, but the modern world of politics has presented and does present still more of them with the ridiculous and chaotic mess of laws and codes which surround every man from his birth to his death, and even before he is born and after he is dead, in an inextricable network of codes, laws, decrees and regulations which stifle him like the silk-worm in the cocoon.

And every day, experience shows us that our legislators, imbued with this political and social artificiality, do nothing but copy the laws of the most dissimilar peoples, according as the fashion comes from Paris or Berlin,— instead of carefully studying the facts of actual life, the conditions of existence and the interests of the people in their respective countries, in order to adapt their laws to them, laws which—if this is not done—remain, as abundant examples show, dead letters because the reality of the facts of life does not permit them to strike their roots into the social soil and to develop a fruitful life.[62]

On the subject of artificial social constructions, the socialists might say to the individualists: let him who is without sin, cast the first stone.

The true reply is wholly different. Scientific socialism represents a much more advanced phase of socialist thought; it is in perfect harmony with modern, experiential science, and it has completely abandoned the fantastic idea of prophesying, at the present time, what human society will be under the new collectivist organization.

What scientific socialism can affirm and does affirm with mathematical certainty, is that the current, the trajectory, of human evolution is in the general direction pointed out and foreseen by socialism, that is to say, in the direction of a continuously and progressively increasing preponderance of the interests and importance of the species over the interests and importance of the individual—and, therefore, in the direction of a continuous *socialization* of the economic life, and with and in consequence of that, of the juridical, moral and political life.

As to the petty details of the new social edifice, we are unable to foresee them, precisely because the new social edifice will be, and is, a *natural* and *spontaneous* product of human evolution, a product which is already in process of formation, and the general outlines of which are already visible, and not an artificial construction of the imagination of some utopian or idealist.

The situation is the same in the social sciences and the natural sciences. In embryology the celebrated law of Haeckel tells us that the development of the *individual* embryo reproduces in miniature the various forms of development of the animal *species* which have preceded it in the zoological series. But the biologist, by studying a human embryo of a few days' or a few weeks' growth, can not tell whether it will be male or female, and still less whether it will be a strong or a weak individual, phlegmatic or nervous, intelligent or not.

He can only tell the general lines of the future evolution of that individual, and must leave it to time to show the exact character of all the particular details of its personality, which will be developed naturally and spontaneously, in conformity with the hereditary organic conditions and the conditions of the environment in which it will live.

This is what can be and what must be the reply of every socialist. This is the position taken by Bebel in the German *Reichstag*[63] in his reply to those who wish to know at the present time what all the details of the future State will be, and who skilfully profiting by the ingenuity of the socialist romancers, criticize their artificial fantasies which are true in their general outlines, but arbitrary in their details.

It would have been just the same thing if, before the French Revolution,—which, as it were, hatched out the bourgeois world, prepared and matured during the previous evolution,—the nobility and the clergy, the classes then in power, had asked the representatives of the Third Estate—bourgeois by birth, though some aristocrats or priests embraced the cause of the bourgeoisie against the privileges of their caste, as the Marquis de Mirabeau and the Abbé Sieyès—"But what sort of a world will this new world of yours be? Show us first its exact plan, and after that we will decide!"

The Third Estate, the bourgeoisie, would not have been able to answer this question, because it was impossible for them to foresee what the human society of the nineteenth century was to be. But this did not prevent the bourgeois revolution from taking place because it represented the next natural and inevitable phase of an eternal evolution. This is now the position of socialism with relation to the bourgeois world. And if this bourgeois world, born only about a century ago, is destined to have a much shorter historical cycle than the feudal (aristocratico-clerical) world, this is simply because the marvelous scientific progress of the nineteenth century has increased a hundred-fold the rapidity of life in time and has nearly annihilated space, and, therefore, civilized humanity traverses now in ten years the same road that it took, in the Middle Ages, a century or two to travel.

The continuously accelerated velocity of human evolution is also one of the laws established and proved by modern social science.

It is the artificial constructions of sentimental socialism which have given birth to the idea—correct so far as they are concerned—that *socialism* is synonymous with *tyranny*.

It is evident that if the new social organization is not the spontaneous form naturally produced by the human evolution, but rather an artificial construction that has issued complete in every detail from the brain of some social architect, the latter will be unable to avoid regulating the new social machinery by an infinite number of rules and by the superior authority which he will assign to a controlling intelligence, either individual or collective. It is easy to understand then, how such an organization gives rise in its opponents—who see in the individualist world only the advantages of liberty, and who forget the evils which so copiously flow from it—the impression of a system of monastic or military discipline.[64]

Another contemporary artificial product has contributed to confirm this impression—*State Socialism*. At bottom, it does not differ from sentimental or utopian socialism, and as Liebknecht said at the socialist congress of Berlin (1892), it would be "a State Capitalism which would join political slavery to economic exploitation." State Socialism is a symptom of the irresistible power of scientific and democratic socialism—as is shown by the famous *rescripts* of Emperor William convoking an international conference to solve (this is the infantile idea of the decree) the problems of labor, and the famous Encyclical on "The Condition of Labor" of the very able Pope, Leo XIII, who has handled the subject with great tact and cleverness.[65] But these imperial rescripts and these papal encyclicals— because it is impossible to leap over or suppress the phases of the social evolution—could only result abortively in our bourgeois, individualist and *laissez faire* world. Certainly it would not have been displeasing to this bourgeois world to see the vigorous contemporary socialism strangled to death in the amorous embraces of official artificiality and of State Socialism, for it had become evident in Germany and elsewhere, that neither laws nor repressive measures of any kind could kill it.[66]

All that arsenal of rules and regulations and provisions for inspection and superintendence has nothing in common with scientific socialism which foresees clearly that the executive guidance of the new social organization will be no more confused than is the present administration of the State, the provinces and the communes, and will, on the contrary, be much better adapted to subserve the interests of both society and the individual, since it will be a natural product and not a parasitic product of the new social organization. Just so, the nervous system of a mammal is the regulating apparatus of its organism; it is, certainly, more complex than that of the organism of a fish or of a mollusc, but it has not, for that reason, tyrannically stifled the autonomy of the other organs and anatomical machinery, or of the cells in their living confederation.

It is understood, then, that to refute socialism, something more is needed than the mere repetition of the current objections against that artificial and sentimental socialism which still continues to exist, I confess, in the nebulous mass of popular ideas. But every day it is losing ground before the intelligent partisans—workingmen, middle-class or aristocrats—of scientific socialism which armed—thanks to the impulse received from the genius of Marx—with all the best-established inductions of modern science, is triumphing over the old objections which our adversaries, through force of mental custom, still repeat, but which have long been left behind by contemporary thought, together with the utopian socialism which provoked them.

The same reply must be made to the second part of the objection, with regard to the mode by which the advent of socialism will be accomplished.

One of the inevitable and logical consequences of utopian and artificial socialism is to think that the architectonic construction proposed by such or such a reformer, ought to be and can be put into practice in a single day by a decree.

In this sense it is quite true that the utopian illusion of empirical socialism is in opposition to the scientific law of evolution, and, *looked at in this way*, I combatted it in my book on *Socialismo e Criminalità*, because at that time (1883) the ideas of scientific or Marxian socialism were not yet generally disseminated in Italy.

A political party or a scientific theory are natural products which must pass through the vital phases of infancy and youth, before reaching complete development. It was, then, inevitable that, before becoming scientific or *positif* (fact-founded), socialism, in Italy as in other countries, should pass through the infantile phases of clannish exclusiveness—the era when socialism was confined to organizations of *manual* laborers—and of nebulous romanticism which, as it gives to the word *revolution* a narrow and incomplete meaning, is always fed with false hope by the illusion that a social organism can be radically changed in a single day with four rifle-shots, just as a monarchical regime could thus be converted into a republican regime.

But it is infinitely easier to change the political envelope of a social organization,—because such a change has little effect on the economic foundation of the social life,—than to completely revolutionize this social life in its economic constitution.

The processes of social transformation, as well as—under various names—those of every sort of transformation in living organisms are: evolution,—revolution,—rebellion,—individual violence.

A mineral or vegetable or animal species may pass through, during the cycle of its existence, these four processes.

As long as the structure and the volume of the centre of crystallization, the germ, or the embryo, increase gradually, we have a gradual and continuous process of *evolution*, which must be followed at a definite stage by a process of *revolution*, more or less prolonged, represented, for example, by the separation of the entire crystal from the mineral mass which surrounds it, or by certain revolutionary phases of vegetable or animal life, as, for example, the moment of sexual reproduction; there may also be a period of *rebellion*, that is to say, of organized personal violence, a frequent and well-verified phenomenon among those species of animals who live in societies; there may also be isolated instances of *personal violence*, as in the struggles to obtain food or for possession of the females between animals of the same species.

These same processes also occur in the human world. By *evolution* must be understood the transformation that takes place day by day, which is almost unnoticed, but continuous and inevitable; by *revolution*, the critical and decisive period, more or less prolonged, of an evolution that has reached its concluding phase; by *rebellion*, the partially collective violence which breaks out, upon the occasion of some particular circumstance, at a definite place and time; and by *individual violence*, the action of one individual against one or several others, which may be the effect of a fanatical passion or of criminal instincts, or the manifestation of a lack of mental equilibrium,—and which identifies itself with the political or religious ideas most in vogue at the moment.

It must be remarked, in the first place, that while revolution and evolution are normal functions of social physiology, rebellion and individual violence are symptoms of social pathology.

These are, nevertheless, merely natural and spontaneous processes, since, as Virchow has shown, pathology is merely the sequel of normal physiology. Besides, the pathological symptoms have, or should have, a great diagnostical value for the classes in power; but the latter, unfortunately, in every period of history, in times of political crisis, as in those of social crisis, have shown themselves unable to conceive of any other remedy than brutal repression—the guillotine or the prison—and they fancy that thus they can cure the organic and constitutional disease which vexes the social body.[67]

But it is indisputable, at all events, that the normal processes of social transformation (and because they are normal, the most fruitful and the surest, although the slowest and the least effective in appearance) are evolution and revolution, using the latter term in its accurate and scientific sense, as the concluding phase of an evolution, and not in the current and incorrect sense of a stormy and violent revolt.[68]

It is evident, in fact, that Europe and America are, in these closing years of the nineteenth century, in a period of revolution, prepared by the evolution begotten by the bourgeois organization itself and promoted by utopian socialism as well as by scientific socialism. Likewise, we are in that period of social life which Bagehot calls "the age of discussion,"[69] and already we can see what Zola has called, in *Germinal*, the cracking of the politico-social crust, and, in fact, all those symptoms which Taine has described in his *l'Ancien Régime*, in relating the history of the twenty years which preceded 1789. As repressive methods are of no avail against domestic revolution, and only serve to expose the symptoms, there can be nothing efficacious and productive of good results, except laws of social reform and preparation which, while safe-guarding the present society, will render less painful, as Marx said, "the birth of the new society."

In this sense, evolution and revolution constitute the most fruitful and surest processes of social metamorphosis. As human society forms a natural and living organism, like all other organisms, it can not endure sudden transformations, as those imagine who think that recourse must be had only or by preference to rebellion or personal violence to inaugurate a new social organization. This seems to me like imagining that a child or a youth could, in a single day, accomplish a biological evolution and become forthwith an adult.[70]

It is easy to understand how a man out of work, in the horrors of starvation, his brain giving way for want of nourishment, may fancy that by giving a policeman a blow with his fist, by throwing a bomb, by raising a barricade, or by taking part in a riot, he is hastening the realization of a social ideal, from which injustice will have vanished.

And, even apart from such cases, it is possible to understand how the power of impulsive feeling, the dominant factor in some natures, may, through a generous impatience, lead them to make some real attempt—and not imaginary like those which the police in all times and all countries prosecute in the courts—to spread terror among those who feel the political or economic power slipping from their hands.

But scientific socialism, especially in Germany, under the direct influence of Marxism, has completely abandoned those old methods of revolutionary romanticism. Though they have often been employed, they have always resulted abortively, and for that very reason the ruling classes no longer dread them, since they are only light, localized assaults on a fortress which still has more than sufficient resistant power to remain victorious and by this victory to retard temporarily the evolution by removing from the scene the strongest and boldest adversaries of the *status quo*.

Marxian socialism is revolutionary in the scientific meaning of the word, and it is now developing into open social revolution—no one will attempt to deny, I think, that the close of the nineteenth century marks the critical phase of the bourgeois evolution rushing under a full head of steam, even in Italy, along the road of individualist capitalism.

Marxian socialism has the candor to say, through the mouths of its most authoritative spokesmen, to the great suffering host of the modern proletariat, that it has no magic wand to transform the world in a single day, as one shifts the scenes in a theatre; it says on the contrary, repeating the prophetic exhortation of Marx, "*Proletarians of all countries, unite*," that the social revolution can not achieve its object, unless it first becomes a vivid fact in the minds of the workers themselves by virtue of the clear perception of their class-interests and of the strength which their union will give them, and that they will not wake up some day under a full-fledged socialist regime, because divided and apathetic for 364 days out of the year they shall rebel on the 365th, or devote themselves to the perpetration of some deed of personal violence.

This is what I call the psychology of the "*gros lot*" (the capital prize in a lottery, etc.). Many workingmen imagine, in fact, that—without doing anything to form themselves into a class-conscious party—they will win some day the capital prize, the social revolution, just as the manna is said to have come down from heaven to feed the Hebrews.

Scientific socialism has pointed out that the transforming power decreases as we descend the scale from one process to another, that of revolution being less than that of evolution, and that of rebellion being less than that of revolution, and individual violence having the least of all. And since it is a question of a complete transformation and, consequently, in its juridical, political and ethical organization, the process of transformation is more effective and better adapted to the purpose in proportion as its *social* character predominates over its *individual* character.

The individualist parties are individualists even in the daily struggle; socialism, on the contrary, is collectivist even in that, because it knows that the present organization does not depend upon the will of such or such an individual, but upon society as a whole. And this is also one reason why charity, however generous it be, being necessarily personal and partial, can not be a remedy for the social, and thereby collective, question of the distribution of wealth.

In political questions, which leave the economico-social foundation untouched, it is possible to understand how, for instance, the exile of Napoleon III. or of the Emperor Don Pedro could inaugurate a republic. But this transformation does not extend to the foundation of the social life, and the German Empire or the Italian Monarchy are, socially, bourgeois just the same as the French Republic or the North American Republic, because notwithstanding the *political* differences between them, they all belong to the same *economico-social* phase.

This is why the processes of evolution and revolution—the only wholly social or collective processes—are the most efficacious, while partial rebellion and, still more, individual violence have only a very feeble power of social transformation; they are, moreover, anti-social and anti-human, because they re-awaken the primitive savage instincts, and because they deny, in the very *person* whom they strike down, the principle with which they believe themselves animated—the principle of respect for human life and of solidarity.

What is the use of hypnotizing oneself with phrases about "the propaganda of the deed" and "immediate action?"

It is known that anarchists, individualists, "amorphists" and "libertarians" admit as a means of social transformation *individual violence* which extends from homicide to theft or *estampage*, even among "companions;" and this is then merely a political coloring given to criminal instincts which must not be confounded with political fanaticism, which is a very different phenomenon, common to the extreme and romantic parties of all times. A scientific examination of each case by itself, with the aid of anthropology and psychology, alone can decide whether the perpetrator of such or such a deed of violence is a congenital criminal, a criminal through insanity, or a criminal through stress of political fanaticism.

I have, in fact, always maintained, and I still maintain, that the "political criminal," whom some wish to class in a special category, does not constitute a peculiar anthropological variety, but that he can be placed under one or another of the anthropological categories of criminals of ordinary law, and particularly one of these three: the *born* criminal having a congenital tendency to crime, the *insane*-criminal, the criminal by stress of fanatical *passion*.

The history of the past and of these latter times afford us obvious illustrations of these several categories.

In the Middle Ages religious beliefs filled the minds of all and colored the criminal or insane excesses of many of the unbalanced. A similar insanity was the efficient cause of the more or less hysterical "sanctity" of some of the saints. At the close of our century it is the politico-social questions which absorb (and with what overwhelming interest!) the universal consciousness—which is stimulated by that universal contagion created by journalism with its great sensationalism—and these are the questions which color the criminal or insane excesses of many of the unbalanced, or which are the determining causes of instances of fanaticism occurring in men who are thoroughly honorable, but afflicted with excessive sensibility.

It is the most extreme form of these politico-social questions which, in each historical period, possesses the most intense suggestive power. In Italy sixty years ago it was *Mazzinnianisme* or *Carbonarisme*; twenty years ago, it was *socialism*; now it is *anarchism*.

It is very easy to understand how there occurred in each period, in accordance with their respective dominant tendencies, deeds of personal violence.... Felice Orsini, for example, is one of the martyrs of the Italian Revolution.

In each case of individual violence, unless one is content with the necessarily erroneous judgments begotten by emotion to reach a correct decision it is necessary to make a physio-psychical examination of the perpetrator, just as it is in the case of any other crime.

Felice Orsini was a political criminal through *passion*. Among the anarchist bomb-throwers or assassins of our day may be found the born criminal— who simply colors his congenital lack of the moral or social sense with a political varnish—; the insane-criminal or mattoid whose mental deficiency becomes blended with the political ideas of the period; and also the criminal through political *passion*, acting from sincere conviction and mentally almost normal, in whom the criminal action is determined (or caused) solely by the false idea (which socialism combats) of the possibility of effecting a *social* transformation by means of *individual* violence.[71]

But no matter whether the particular crime is that of a congenital criminal or of a madman or of a political criminal through passion, it is none the less true that personal violence, as adopted by the anarchist individualists, is simply the logical product of individualism carried to extremes and, therefore, the natural product of the existing economic organization— though its production is also favored by the "delirium of hunger," acute or chronic; but it is also the least efficacious and the most anti-human means of social transformation.[72]

But all anarchists are not individualists, *amorphists* or autonomists; there are also anarchist-communists.

The latter repudiates deeds of *personal violence*, as ordinary means of social transformation (Merlino, for example has recently stated this in his pamphlet: *Necessità e base di un accordo*, Prato, 1892), but even these anarchist-communists cut themselves off from Marxian socialism, both by their ultimate *ideal* and more especially by their *method* of social transformation. They combat Marxian socialism because it is *law-abiding* and *parliamentary*, and they contend that the most efficacious and the surest mode of social transformation is *rebellion*.

These assertions which respond to the vagueness of the sentiments and ideas of too large a portion of the working-class and to the impatience provoked by their wretched condition, may meet with a temporary, unintelligent approval, but their effect can be only ephemeral. The explosion of a bomb may indeed give birth to a momentary emotion, but it can not advance by the hundredth part of an inch the evolution in men's minds toward socialism, while it causes a reaction in feeling, a reaction in part sincere, but skilfully fomented and exploited as a pretext for repression.

To say to the laborers that, without having made ready the requisite material means, but especially without solidarity and without an intelligent conception of the goal and without a high moral purpose, they ought to rise against the classes in power, is really to play into the hands of those very classes, since the latter are sure of the material victory when the evolution is not ripe and the revolution is not ready.[73]

And so it has been possible to show in the case of the late Sicilian rebellion, in spite of all the lies of those interested in hiding the truth, that in those districts where socialism was most advanced and best understood there were no deeds of personal violence, no revolts, as, for example, among the peasants of Piana dei Greci, of whom Nicola Barbato had made intelligent socialists; while those convulsive movements occurred outside of the field of the socialist propaganda as a rebellion against the exactions of the local governments and of the *camorre*,[74] or in those districts where the socialist propaganda was less intelligent and was stifled by the fierce passions caused by hunger and misery.[75]

History demonstrates that the countries where revolts have been the most frequent are those in which social progress is the least advanced. The popular energies exhaust and destroy themselves in these feverish, convulsive excesses, which alternate with periods of discouragement and despair—which are the fitting environment of the Buddhist theory of *electoral abstention*—a very convenient theory for the conservative parties. In such countries we never see that continuity of premeditated action, slower and less effective in appearance, but in reality the only kind of action that can accomplish those things which appear to us as the miracles of history.

Therefore Marxian socialism in all countries has proclaimed that from this time forth the principal means of social transformation must be *the conquest of the public powers* (in local administrations as well as in national Parliaments) as one of the results of the organization of the laborers into a class-conscious party. The further the political organization of the laborers, in civilized countries, shall progress, the more one will see realized, by a resistless evolution, the socialist organization of society, at first by partial concessions, but ever growing more important, wrested from the capitalist class by the working-class (the law restricting the working-day to Eight Hours, for example), and then by the complete transformation of individual ownership into social ownership.

As to the question whether this complete transformation, which is at present being prepared for by a process of gradual evolution which is nearing the critical and decisive period of the social revolution, can be accomplished without the aid of other means of transformation—such as rebellion and individual violence—this is a question which no one can answer in advance. Marxian socialists are not prophets.

Our sincere wish is that the social revolution, when its evolution shall be ripe, may be effected peacefully, as so many other revolutions have been, without blood-shed—like the English Revolution, which preceded by a century, with its *Bill of Rights*, the French Revolution; like the Italian Revolution in Tuscany in 1859; like the Brazilian Revolution, with the exile of the Emperor Dom Pedro, in 1892.

It is certain that socialism by spreading education and culture among the people, by organizing the workers into a class-conscious party under its banner, is only increasing the probability of the fulfilment of our hope, and is dissipating the old forebodings of a *reaction* after the advent of socialism, which were indeed justified when socialism was still utopian in its means of realization instead of being, as it now is, a natural and spontaneous, and therefore inevitable and irrevocable, phase of the evolution of humanity.

Where will this social revolution start? I am firmly convinced that if the Latin peoples, being Southerners, are more ready for revolt, which may suffice for purely political transformations, the peoples of the North, the Germans and Anglo-Saxons are better prepared for the tranquil and orderly but inexorable process of the true revolution, understood as the critical phase of an organic, incomplete, preparatory evolution, which is the only effective process for a truly social transformation.

It is in Germany and England, where the greater development of bourgeois industrialism inevitably aggravates its detrimental consequences, and thereby magnifies the necessity for socialism, that the great social metamorphosis will perhaps being—though indeed it has begun everywhere—and from there it will spread across old Europe, just as at the close of the last century the signal for the political and bourgeois revolution was raised by France.

However this may be, we have just demonstrated once more the profound difference there is between socialism and anarchism—which our opponents and the servile press endeavor to confound[76] and, at all events, I have demonstrated that Marxian socialism is in harmony with modern science and is its logical continuation. That is exactly the reason why it has made the theory of evolution the basis of its inductions and why it thus marks the truly living and final phase—and, therefore, the only phase recognized by the intelligence of the collectivist democracy—of socialism which had theretofore remained floating in the nebulosities of sentiment and why it has taken as its guide the unerring compass of scientific thought, rejuvenated by the works of Darwin and Spencer.

FOOTNOTES:

[62] We have a typical example of this in the new Italian penal code, which, as I said before its enforcement, shows no signs of special adaptation to Italian conditions.

It might just as well be a code made for Greece or Norway, and it has borrowed from the countries of the north the system of confinement in cells, which even then in the north was recognized in all its costly absurdity as a system devised for the brutalization of men.

[63] BEBEL, *Zukunftstaat und Sozialdemokratie*, 1893.

[64] It is this artificial socialism which Herbert Spencer attacks.

[65] See "Socialism: a Reply to the Pope's Encyclical," by Robert Blatchford. The International Publishing Co., New York.—Tr.

[66] To this State socialism apply most of the individualist and anarchist objections of Spencer In "*Man vs. State.*" D. Appleton & Co., New York.

You will recall on this subject the celebrated debate between Spencer and Laveleye: "The State and the Individual or Social Darwinism and Christianity," in the "Contemporary Review," 1885.

Lafargue has also replied to Spencer, but has not pointed out the fact that Spencer's criticisms apply, not to democratic socialism, our socialism, but to State socialism.

See also CICCOTTI on this subject.

[67] At the moment when I was correcting the proofs of the Italian edition of this work, M. Crispi had just proposed the "exceptional laws for the public safety," which, using the outrages of the anarchists as a pretext, aimed by this method to strike a blow at and to suppress socialism.

Repressive laws can suppress men, but not ideas. Has the failure of the exceptional laws against the socialist party in Germany been forgotten?

It is possible to increase the number of crimes, to suppress public liberties ... but that is no remedy. Socialism will continue its forward march just the same.

[68] LOMBROSO and LASCHI, *Le Crime politique*, etc., and the monograph of ELISEE RECLUS, Evolution et Révolution.

[69] WALTER BAGEHOT, Physics and Politics. D. Appleton & Co.

[70] It is this lack of even elementary knowledge of geology, biology, etc., which makes the vague ideal of anarchy so attractive to many men or the people with really bright minds, but with no scientific training, even though they repudiate the employment of violent methods.

In my opinion a more wide-spread instruction in the natural sciences— together with their substitution for the classics—would do more than any repressive laws to suppress the outrages of anarchy.

[71] HAMON, *Les Hommes et les théories de l'anarchie*, Paris, 1893.— LOMBROSO, *Ultime scoperte ed applicazioni dell' antropologia criminale*, Turin, 1893.

[72] At the moment when I was correcting the proofs of the Italian edition of this book, the emotion had not yet subsided which grew out of the harmless attack upon Crispi, at Rome, on the 16th of June, and especially the much keener emotion produced by the death of the President of the French Republic, Sadi Carnot, on the 24th of June.

I reproduce here, as documentary evidence, the declaration published by a section of the *Socialist Party of Italian Workers* in the *Secolo* of the 27-28 June, and distributed by thousands in Milan as a manifesto, and which was not mentioned by either the Conservative or the Progressive newspapers, who tried by their silence to perpetuate the confusion between socialism and anarchy.

Here is the declaration:

> *The Socialist Party to the Workingmen of Italy.*—Down with assassins! "Humanity now understands that life is sacred, and does not tolerate brutal violations of this great principle which is morally the soul of socialism."
>
> C. PRAMPOLINI.
>
> "He who struggles for the right to life, in exchange for his labor, condemns every assault upon human life,—whether it be the work of bourgeois exploitation in factories, or of the bombs or daggers of unintelligent revolutionists.
>
> "The Socialist Party which has this principle for a shibboleth, which expects everything from the class-conscious organization of the working class, execrates the crime committed against the person of the President of the French Republic, as a brutal deed, as the negation of every principle of revolutionary logic.
>
> "It is necessary to arouse in the proletariat the consciousness of their own rights, to furnish them the *structure* of organization, and to induce them to *function* as a new organism. It is necessary to conquer the public powers by the means which modern civilization gives us.
>
> "To revolt, to throw at haphazard a bomb among the spectators in a theatre, or to kill an individual, is the act of barbarians or of ignorant people. The *Socialist Party* sees in such deeds the violent manifestation of *bourgeois* sentiments.
>
> "We are the adversaries of all the violences of bourgeois exploitation, of the guillotine, of musketry discharges (aimed at strikers, etc.), and of anarchist outrages. *Hurrah for Socialism!*"

Socialism represses all these sterile and repugnant forms of individual violence.

Carnot's death accomplished nothing except to arouse a transitory atavistic hatred of Italians. Afterward, the French Republic elected another

President and everything was as before. The same may be said of Russia after the assassination of Alexander II.

But the question may be regarded from another point of view, which the conservatives, the progressives and the radicals too completely forget.

The very day of these outrages two explosions of gas took place, one in the mines of Karwinn (Austria), and the other in the mines of Cardiff (England); the first *caused the death of 257 miners* ..., the second *the death of 210!!*

Although the death of an honorable man, like Carnot, may be regretted, it is not to be compared to the mass of human sufferings, misery and woe which fell upon these 467 working-class *families*, equally innocent as he.

It will be said, it is true, that the murder of Carnot was the *voluntary* act of a fanatic, while no one directly killed these 467 miners!—And certainly this is a difference.

But it must be remarked that if the death of these 467 miners is not *directly* the voluntary work of any one, it is *indirectly* a result of individual capitalism, which, to swell its revenues, reduces expenses to the lowest possible point, does not curtail the hours of labor, and does not take all the *preventive* measures indicated by science and sometimes even enjoined by law, which is in such cases not respected, for the justice of every country is as flexible to accommodate the interests of the ruling class as it is rigid when applied against the interests of the working-class.

If the mines were collectively owned, it is certain the owners would be less stingy about taking all the technical preventive precautions (electric lighting, for instance), which would diminish the number of these frightful catastrophes which infinitely increase the anonymous multitude of the martyrs of toil and which do not even trouble the digestion of the *share-holders* in mining companies.

That is what the individualist regime gives us; all this will be transformed by the socialist regime.

[73] RIENZI, *l'Anarchisme*; DEVILLE, *l'Anarchisme*.

[74] A. ROSSI, *l'Agitazione in Sicilia*, Milan, 1894. COLAJANNI, *In Sicilia*, Rome, 1894.

[75] The *camorre* were tyrannical secret societies that were formerly prevalent and powerful in Italy.—Translator.

[76] I must recognize that one of the recent historians of socialism, *M. l'Abbé Winterer*—more candid and honorable than more than one jesuitical journalist—distinguishes always, in each country, the *socialist* movement from the *anarchist* movement.

WINTERER, *le Socialisme contemporain*, Paris, 1894, 2nd edition.

PART THIRD.

SOCIOLOGY AND SOCIALISM.

XIII.

THE STERILITY OF SOCIOLOGY.

One of the strangest facts in the history of the scientific thought of the nineteenth century is that, though the profound scientific revolution caused by Darwinism and Spencerian evolution has reinvigorated with new youth all the physical, biological and even psychological sciences, when it reached the domain of the social sciences, it only superficially rippled the tranquil and orthodox surface of the lake of that social science *par excellence*, political economy.

It has led, it is true, through the initiative of Auguste Comte—whose name has been somewhat obscured by those of Darwin and Spencer, but who was certainly one of the greatest and most prolific geniuses of our age—to the creation of a new science, *Sociology*, which should be, together with the natural history of human societies, the crowning glory of the new scientific edifice erected by the experimental method.

I do not deny that sociology, in the department of purely descriptive anatomy of the social organism, has made great and fruitful new contributions to contemporary science, even developing into some specialized branches of sociology, of which *criminal sociology*, thanks to the labors of the Italian school, has become one of the most important results.

But when the politico-social question is entered upon, the new science of sociology is overpowered by a sort of hypnotic sleep and remains suspended in a sterile, colorless limbo, thus permitting sociologists to be in public economy, as in politics, conservatives or radicals, in accordance with their respective whims or subjective tendencies.

And while Darwinian biology, by the scientific determination of the relations between the individual and the species, and evolutionist sociology itself by describing in human society the organs and the functions of a new organism, was making the individual a cell in the animal organism, Herbert Spencer was loudly proclaiming his English individualism extending to the most absolute theoretical anarchism.

A period of stagnation was inevitable in the scientific productive activity of sociology, after the first original observations in descriptive social anatomy and in the natural history of human societies. Sociology represented thus a sort of arrested development in experimental scientific thought, because those who cultivated it, wittingly or unwittingly, recoiled before the logical and radical conclusions that the modern scientific revolution was destined to establish in the social domain—the most important domain of all if science was to become the handmaid of life, instead of contenting itself with that barren formula, science for the sake of science.

The secret of this strange phenomenon consists not only in the fact that, as Malagodi said,[77] sociology is still in the period of scientific *analysis* and not yet in that of *synthesis*, but especially in the fact that the logical consequences of Darwinism and of scientific evolutionism applied to the study of human society lead inexorably to socialism, as I have demonstrated in the foregoing pages.

FOOTNOTE:

[77] MALAGODI, *Il Socialismo e la scienza.* In *Critica Sociale*, Aug. 1, 1892.

XIV.

MARX COMPLETES DARWIN AND SPENCER.
CONSERVATIVES AND SOCIALISTS.

To Karl Marx is due the honor of having scientifically formulated these logical applications of experiential science to the domain of social economy. Beyond doubt, the exposition of these truths is surrounded, in his writings, with a multitude of technical details and of apparently dogmatic formulæ, but may not the same be said of the FIRST PRINCIPLES of Spencer, and are not the luminous passages on *evolution* in it surrounded with a dense fog of abstractions on time, space, the unknowable, etc.? Until these last few years a vain effort was made to consign, by a conspiracy of silence, the masterly work of Marx to oblivion, but now his name is coming to rank with those of Charles Darwin and Herbert Spencer as the three Titans of the scientific revolution which begot the intellectual renaissance and gave fresh potency to the civilizing thought of the latter half of the nineteenth century.

The ideas by which the genius of Karl Marx completed in the domain of social economy the revolution effected by science are in number three.

The first is the discovery of the law of surplus-labor. This law gives us a scientific explanation of the accumulation of private property not created by the labor of the accumulator; as this law has a more peculiarly technical character, we will not lay further stress upon it here, as we have given a general idea of it in the preceding pages.

The two other Marxian theories are more directly related to our observations on scientific socialism, since they undoubtedly furnish us the sure and infallible key to the life of society.

I allude, first, to the idea expressed by Marx, as long ago as 1859, in his *Critique de l'économie politique*, that the economic phenomena form the foundation and the determining conditions of all other human or social manifestations, and that, consequently, ethics, law and politics are only derivative phenomena determined by the economic factor, in accordance with the conditions of each particular people in every phase of history and under all climatic conditions.

This idea which corresponds to that great biological law which states the dependence of the function on the nature and capacities of the organ and which makes each individual the result of the innate and acquired conditions of his physiological organism, living in a given environment, so that a biological application may be given to the famous saying: "Tell me what you eat and I will tell you what you are,"—this sublime idea which unfolds before our eyes the majestic drama of history, no longer as the arbitrary succession of great men on the stage of the social theatre, but rather as the resultant of the economic conditions of each people, this sublime idea, after having been partially applied by Thorold Rogers[78] has been so brilliantly expounded and illustrated by Achille Loria,[79] that I believe it unnecessary to say anything more about it.

One idea, however, still appears to me necessary to complete this Marxian theory, as I remarked in the first edition of my book: *Socialismo e criminalità*.

It is necessary, indeed, to rid this impregnable theory of that species of narrow dogmatism with which it is clothed in Marx and still more in Loria.

It is perfectly true that every phenomenon, as well as every institution— moral, juridical or political—is simply the result of the economic phenomena and conditions of the transitory physical and historical environment. But, as a consequence of that law of natural causality which tells us that every effect is always the resultant of numerous concurrent causes and not of one cause alone, and that every effect becomes in its turn a cause of other phenomena, it is necessary to amend and complete the too rigid form that has been given to this true idea.

Just as all the psychical manifestations of the individual are the resultant of the organic conditions (temperament) and of the environment in which he lives, in the same way, all the social manifestations—moral, juridical or political—of a people are the resultant of their organic conditions (race) and of the environment, as these are the determining causes of the given economic organization which is the physical basis of life.

In their turn, the individual psychical conditions become causes and effect, although with less power, the individual organic conditions and the issue of the struggle for life. In the same way, the moral, juridical and political institutions, from effects become causes (there is, in fact, for modern science no *substantial* difference between cause and effect, except that the effect is always the latter of two related phenomena, and the cause always the former) and react in their turn, although with less efficacy, on the economic conditions.

An individual who has studied the laws of hygiene may influence beneficently, for instance, the imperfections of his digestive apparatus, but always within the very narrow limits of his organic capacities. A scientific discovery, an electoral law may have an effect on industry or on the conditions of labor, but always within limits fixed by the framework of the fundamental economic organization. This is why moral, juridical and political institutions have a greater influence on the relations between the various subdivisions of the class controlling the economic power (capitalists, industrial magnates, landed proprietors) than on the relations between the capitalist—property-owners on the one side and the toilers on the other.

It suffices here for me to have mentioned this Marxian law and I will refer to the suggestive book of Achille Loria the reader who desires to see how this law scientifically explains all the phenomena, from the most trivial to the most imposing, of the social life. This law is truly the most scientific and the most prolific sociological theory that has ever been discovered by the genius of man. It furnishes, as I have already remarked, a scientific, physiological, experiential explanation of social history in the most magnificent dramas as well as of personal history in its most trivial episodes—on explanation in perfect harmony with the entire trend—which has been described as materialistic—of modern scientific thought.[80]

If we leave out of consideration the two unscientific explanations of free will and divine providence, we find that two one-sided and therefore incomplete, although correct and scientific, explanations of human history have been given. I refer to the *physical determinism* of Montesquieu, Buckle and Metschnikoff, and to the *anthropological determinism* of the ethnologists who find the explanation of the events of history in the organic and psychical characteristics of the various races of men.

Karl Marx sums up, combines and completes these two theories by his *economic determinism*.

The economic conditions—which are the resultant of the *ethnical* energies and aptitudes acting in a given *physical* environment—are the determining basis of all the moral, juridical and political phenomenal manifestations of human life, both individual and social.

This is the sublime conception, the fact-founded and scientific Marxian theory, which fears no criticism, resting as it does on the best established results of geology and biology, of psychology and sociology.

It is thanks to it that students of the philosophy of law and sociology are able to determine the true nature and functions of the *State* which, as it is nothing but "society juridically and politically organized," is only the secular arm used by the class in possession of the economic power—and consequently of the political, juridical and administrative power—to preserve their own special privileges and to postpone as long as possible the evil day when they must surrender them.

The other sociological theory by which Karl Marx has truly dissipated the clouds which had ere then darkened the sky of the aspirations of socialism, and which has supplied scientific socialism with a political compass by the use of which it can guide its course, with complete confidence and certainty, in the struggles of every-day life, is the great historical law of *class struggles*.[81] ("The history of all hitherto existing society is the history of class struggles." Communist Manifesto. Marx and Engels. 1848.)

If it is granted that the economic conditions of social groups, like those of individuals, constitute the fundamental, determining cause of all the moral, juridical and political phenomena, it is evident that every social group, every individual will be led to act in accordance with its or his economic interest, because the latter is the physical basis of life and the essential condition of all other development. In the political sphere, each social class will be inclined to pass laws, to establish institutions and to perpetuate customs and beliefs which, directly or indirectly subserve its interests.

These laws, these institutions, these beliefs, handed down by inheritance or tradition, finally obscure or conceal their economic origin, and philosophers and jurists and often even the laity defend them as truths, subsisting by virtue of their own intrinsic merits, without seeing their real source, but the latter—the economic sub-stratum—is none the less the only scientific explanation of these laws, institutions and beliefs. And in this fact consists the greatness and strength of the perspicacious conception of the genius of Marx.[82]

As in the modern world there are now but two classes, with subordinate varieties,—on the one side the workers to whatever category they belong, and on the other the property owners who do not work,—the socialist theory of Marx leads us to this evident conclusion: since political parties are merely the echoes and the mouth-pieces of class interests—no matter what the subvarieties of these classes may be—there can be substantially only two political parties: the socialist labor party and the individualist party of the class in possession of the land and the other means of production.

The difference in the character of the economic monopoly may cause, it is true, a certain diversity of political *color*, and I have always contended that the great landed proprietors represent the conservative tendencies of political stagnation, while the holders of financial or industrial capital represent in many instances the progressive party, driven by its own nature to petty innovations of form, while finally those who possess only an intellectual capital, the liberal professions, etc., may go to the extreme length of political radicalism.

On the vital question—that is to say on the economic question of property—conservatives, progressives and radicals are all individualists. On this point they are all, in their essential nature of the same social class and, in spite of certain sentimental sympathies, the adversaries of the working class and of those who, although born on *the other shore*, have embraced the political programme of that class, a programme necessarily corresponding to the primordial economic necessity—that is to say, the socialization of the land and the means of production with all the innumerable and radical moral, juridical and political transformations, which this socialization will inevitably bring to pass in the social world.

This is why contemporary political life cannot but degenerate into the most sterile *byzantinisme* and the most corrupt strife for bribes and spoils, when it is confined to the superficial skirmishes between individualist parties, which differ only by a shade and in their formal names, but whose ideas are so similar that one often sees radicals and progressives less modern than many conservatives.

There will be a new birth of political life only with the development of the socialist party, because, after the disappearance from the political stage of the historical figures of the patriots (the founders of modern Italy) and of the personal reasons which split up the representatives into different political groups, the formation of one single individualist party will become necessary, as I declared in the Italian Chamber on the 20th of December, 1893.

The historical duel will then be begun, and the Class Struggle will then display on the field of politics all its beneficent influence. Beneficent, I say, because the class struggle must be understood not in the contemptible sense of a Saturnalia of fist-fights and outrages, of malevolence and personal violence, but must be worthily conceived as a great social drama. With all my heart I hope that this conflict may be settled, for the progress of civilization, without bloody convulsions, but historical destiny has decreed the conflict, and it is not given to us or to others to avert or postpone it.

It follows from all that we have just said that these ideas of political socialism, because they are scientific, dispose their partisans both to *personal tolerance* and to *theoretical inflexibility*.[83] This is also a conclusion reached by experimental psychology in the domain of philosophy. However great our personal sympathies may be for such or such a representative of the radical faction of the individualist party (as well as for every honorable and sincere representative of any scientific, religious or political opinion whatsoever), we are bound to recognize that there are on the side of socialism no *partiti affini*.[84] It is necessary to be on one side or the other—individualist or socialist. There is no middle ground. And I am constantly growing more and more convinced that the only serviceable tactics for the formation of a socialist party likely to live, is precisely that policy of theoretical inflexibility and of refusing to enter into any "alliance" with *partiti affini*, as such an alliance is for socialism only a "false placenta" for a fetus that is unlikely to live.

The conservative and the socialist are the natural products of the individual character and the social environment. One is born a conservative or an innovator just as one is born a painter or a surgeon. Therefore the socialists have no contempt for or bitterness toward the sincere representatives of any faction of the conservative party, though they combat their ideas unrelentingly. If such or such a socialist shows himself intolerant, if he abuses his opponents, this is because he is the victim of a passing emotion or of an ill-balanced temperament; it is, therefore, very excusable.

The thing that provokes a smile of pity is to see certain conservatives "young in years, but old in thought"—for conservatism in the young can be nothing but the effect of calculating selfishness or the index of psychical anemia—have an air of complacency or of pity for socialists whom they consider, at best, as "misled," without perceiving that what is normal is for the old to be conservatives, but that young conservatives can be nothing but *egoists* who are afraid of losing the life of idle luxury into which they were born or the advantages of the orthodox fashion of dividing (?) the fruits of labor. Their hearts at least, if not their brains, are abnormally small. The socialist, who has everything to lose and nothing to gain by boldly declaring his position and principles, possesses by contrast all the superiority of a disinterested altruism, especially when having been born in the aristocratic or the bourgeois class he has renounced the brilliant pleasure of a life of leisure to defend the cause of the weak and the oppressed.[85]

But, it is said, these bourgeois socialists act in this way through love of popularity! This is a strange form of selfishness, at all events, which prefers to the quickly reaped rewards and profits of bourgeois individualism, "the socialist idealism" of popular sympathy, especially when it might gain this sympathy by other means which would compromise it less in the eyes of the class in power.

Let us hope, in concluding, that when the bourgeoisie shall have to surrender the economic power and the political power in order that they may be used for the benefit of all in the new society and that, as Berenini recently said, victors and vanquished may really become brothers without distinction of class in the common assured enjoyment of a mode of life worthy of human beings, let us hope that in surrendering power, the bourgeoisie will do it with that dignity and self-respect which the aristocracy showed when it was stripped of its class privileges by the triumphant bourgeoisie at the time of the French Revolution.

It is the truth of the message of socialism and its perfect agreement with the most certain inductions of experimental science which explain to us not only its tremendous growth and progress, which could not be merely the purely negative effect of a material and moral malady rendered acute by a period of social crisis, but above all it explains to us that unity of intelligent, disciplined, class-conscious solidarity which presents, in the world-wide celebration of the first of May, a moral phenomenon of such grandeur that human history presents no parallel example, if we except the movement of primitive Christianity which had, however, a much more restricted field of action than contemporary socialism.

Henceforth—disregarding the hysterical or unreasoning attempts to revert from bourgeois scepticism to mysticism as a safeguard against the moral and material crisis of the present time, attempts which make us think of those lascivious women who become pious bigots on growing old[86]— henceforth both partisans and adversaries of socialism are forced to recognize the fact that, like Christianity at the dissolution of the Roman world, Socialism constitutes the only force which restores the hope of a better future to the old and disintegrating human society—a hope no longer begotten by a faith inspired by the unreasoning transports of sentiment, but born of rational confidence in the inductions of modern experimental science.

THE END.

FOOTNOTES:

[78] J. E. TH. ROGERS, The Economic Interpretation of History, London, 1888.

[79] LORIA, *Les Bases économiques de la constitution sociale,* 2nd edition, Paris, 1894. (This work is available in English under the title: "The Economic Foundations of Society." Swan Sonnenschein, London.—Tr.)

To the general idea of Karl Marx, Loria adds a theory about "the occupation of free land," which is the fundamental cause of the technical explanation of the different econo-micro-social organizations, a theory which he has amply demonstrated in his *Analisi della proprietà capitalistica,* Turin, 1892.

[80] It is seen what our judgment must be regarding the thesis maintained by Ziegler, in his book: *La question sociale est une question morale* (The social question is a moral question). French trans., Paris, 1894. Just as psychology is an effect of physiology, so the moral phenomena are effects of the economic facts. Such books are only intended, more or less consciously, to divert attention from the vital point of the question, which is that formulated by Karl Marx.

See on our side, DE GREEF, *l'Empirieme, l'utopié et le socialisme scientifique,* Revue Socialiste, Aug., 1886, p. 688.

[81] As proof of that conspiracy of silence about the theories of Karl Marx, it suffices for me to point out that the historians of socialism generally mention only the technical theory of *surplus-labor,* and ignore the two other laws: (1) the determination of social phenomena and institutions by economic conditions, and (2) the Class Struggle.

[82] The votes on measures imposing taxes in the legislative bodies of all countries afford obvious illustrations of this principle. (The alignment of forces in the struggle for the income tax under the late administration of President Cleveland, is a very striking instance.—Tr.)

[83] If *uncompromisingness* was an English word, it would express the thought more clearly and strongly.—Tr.

[84] Parties related by affinity of object, tactics, or, more especially, of immediate demands.—Tr.

[85] See the lectures of DE AMICIS. *Osservazioni sulla questione sociale,* Lecce, 1894. LABRIOLA, *Il Socialismo,* Rome, 1890. G. OGGERO, *Il Socialismo,* 2nd edition, Milan, 1894.

[86] There are, however, certain forms of this mysticism which appeal to our sympathies very strongly. Such forms I will call *social mysticism*. We may instance the works of Tolstoi, who envelops his socialism with the doctrine of "non-resistance to evil by violent means," drawn from the *Sermon on the Mount.*

Tolstoi is also an eloquent *anti-militarist*, and I am pleased to see quoted in his book *le Salut est en vous*, Paris, 1894, a passage from one of my lectures against war.

But he maintains a position aloof from contemporary experimental science, and his work thus fails to reach the mark.

APPENDIX I[87]

Editor, etc.

DEAR SIR:—

I have read in your journal a letter from Mr. Herbert Spencer in which he, relying on indirect information conveyed to him, regarding my book, *Socialism and Modern Science*, expresses "his astonishment at the audacity of him who has made use *of his name* to defend socialism."

Permit me to say to you that no socialist has ever dreamt of making Mr. Spencer (who is certainly the greatest of living philosophers) pass as a partisan of socialism. It is strange, indeed, that anyone could have been able to make him believe that there is in Italy enough ignorance among writers as well as among readers for one to misuse so grotesquely the name of Herbert Spencer, whose extreme individualism is known to all the world.

But the personal opinion of Herbert Spencer is a quite different thing from the logical consequence of the scientific theories concerning universal evolution, which he has developed more fully and better than anyone else, but of which he has not the official monopoly and whose free expansion by the labor of other thinkers he can not inhibit.

I myself, in the preface of my book, pointed out that Spencer and Darwin stopped half-way on the road to the logical consequences of their doctrines. But I also demonstrated that these very doctrines constituted the scientific foundation of the socialism of Marx, the only one who, by rising above the sentimental socialism of former days, has arranged in a systematic and orderly fashion the facts of the social economy, and by induction drawn from them political conclusions in support of the revolutionary method of tactics as a means of approach to a revolutionary goal.

As regards Darwinism, being unable to repeat here the arguments which are already contained in my book and which will be more fully developed in the second edition, it suffices for me to remind you—since it has been thought fit to resort to arguments having so little weight as appeals to the authority of individuals—that, among many others, the celebrated Virchow foresaw, with great penetration, that Darwinism would lead directly to socialism, and let me remind you that the celebrated Wallace, Darwinian though he is, is a member of the English *League* for the *Nationalization* of the *Land*, which constitutes one of the fundamental conclusions of socialism.[88]

And, from another point of view, what is the famous doctrine of "class-struggle" which Marx revealed as the positive key of human history, but the

Darwinian law of the "struggle for life" transformed from a chaotic strife between individuals to a conflict between collectivities?

Just the same as every individual, every class or social group struggles for its existence. And just as the bourgeoisie struggled against the clergy and the aristocracy, and triumphed in the French Revolution, in the same way to-day the international proletariat struggles, and not by the use of violence, as is constantly charged against us, but by propaganda and organization for its economic and moral existence at present so ill assured and depressed to so sadly low a plane.

As regards the theory of evolution, how can any one not see that it most flagrantly contradicts the classical theories of political economy, which looks upon the basic laws of the existing economic organization as eternal and immutable laws?

Socialism, on the contrary, maintains that the economic institutions and the juridical and political institutions are only the historical product of their particular epoch, and that therefore they are changing, since they are in a state of continuous evolution, which causes the present to differ from the past, just as the future will be different from the present.

Herbert Spencer believes that universal evolution dominates over all orders of phenomena, with the exception of the organization of property, which he declares is destined to exist eternally under its individualistic form. The socialists, on the contrary, believe that the organization of property will inevitably undergo—just as all other institutions—a radical transformation, and, taking into consideration its historical transformations, they show that the economic evolution is marching and will march faster and faster—as a consequence of the increased evils of individualist concentration—toward its goal, the complete socialization of the means of production which constitute the physical basis of the social and collective life, and which must not and can not therefore remain in the hands of a few individuals.

Between these two doctrines it is not difficult to decide which is the more in harmony with the scientific theory of physical and social evolution.

In any case, with all the respect due to our intellectual father, Herbert Spencer, but also with all the pride to which my scientific studies and conscience give me the right, I am content with having repelled the anathema which Herbert Spencer—without having read my book and on indirect and untrustworthy information—has thought proper to hurl with such a dogmatic tone against a scientific thesis which I have affirmed—not merely on the strength of an *ipse dixi* (a mode of argument which has had its day)—but which I have worked out and supported with arguments which have, up to this time, awaited in vain a scientific refutation.

Rome, June, 1895.

FOOTNOTES:

[87] This appendix is a copy of a letter addressed by M. Ferri to an Italian newspaper which had printed a letter addressed by Herbert Spencer to M. Fiorentino.

[88] Wallace has advanced beyond this "half way house," and now calls himself a Socialist.—Tr.

APPENDIX II.[89]

SOCIALIST SUPERSTITION AND INDIVIDUALIST MYOPIA.

Among the numerous publications which, for or against socialism, have appeared in Italy since my *Socialismo e scienza positiva*[90]—which demonstrated the agreement of socialism with the fundamental lines of contemporary scientific thought—the book of Baron Garofalo was looked forward to with eager interest. It received attention both because of the fame of the author and the open and radical disagreement which its publication made manifest in the ranks of the founders of the school of positive criminology, formerly united in such close bonds in the propaganda and defense of the new science—criminal anthropology and sociology—created by M. Lombroso.

It is true that the scientific union between the founders of the new Italian school of criminology formed an alliance, but they were never in perfect unison.

M. Lombroso gave to the study of crime as a natural and social phenomenon the initial impulse, and brilliantly supported the correctness of this conception by his fruitful anthropological and biological investigations. I contributed the systematic, theoretical treatment of the problem of human responsibility, and my psychological and sociological studies enabled me to classify the natural causes of crime and the anthropological categories of criminals. I showed the predominant role of *social* prevention—quite a different thing from police prevention—of criminality, and demonstrated the infinitesimal influence of repression, which is always violent and only acts after the mischief has been done.

M. Garofalo—though he was in accord with us on the subject of the diagnosis of criminal pathology—contributed nevertheless a current of ideas peculiar to himself, ideas more metaphysical and less heterodox; such, for instance, as the idea that the anomaly shown by the criminal is only a "moral anomaly;" that religion has a preventive influence on criminality; that severe repression is, at all events, the effective remedy; that misery (poverty) it not only not the sole and exclusive factor in producing crime (which I always maintained and still maintain), but that it has no determining influence on crime; and that popular education, instead of being a preventive means, is, on the contrary, an incentive, etc.

These ideas, in evident disagreement with the inductions of biology and of criminal psychology and sociology—as I have elsewhere demonstrated—nevertheless did not prevent harmony among the positivists of the new school. In fact, these personal and antiquated conceptions of M. Garofalo passed almost unnoticed. His action was especially notable by reason of the greater importance and development he gave to the purely juridical inductions of the new school, which he systematized into a plan of reforms in criminal law and procedure. He was the jurist of the new school, M. Lombroso was the anthropologist, and I the sociologist.

But while in Lombroso and myself the progressive and heterodox tendency—extending even to socialism—became more and more marked, it could already be foreseen that in M. Garofalo the orthodox and reactionary tendencies would prevail, thus leading us away from that common ground on which we have fought side by side, and might still so fight. For I do not believe that these disagreements concerning the social future must necessarily prevent our agreement on the more limited field of the present diagnosis of a phenomenon of social pathology.

After the explanation of this personal matter, we must now examine the contents of this "*Superstition socialiste*," in order to see, in this schism of the scientific criminologists, which side has followed most systematically the method of experimental science, and traced with the most rigorous exactness the trajectory of human evolution.

We must see who is the more scientific, he who in carrying the experimental science beyond the narrow confines of criminal anthropology and applying it in the broad field of social science, accepts all the logical consequences of scientific observations and gives his open adherence to Marxian socialism—or he who while being a positivist and innovator in one special branch of science, remains a conservative in the other branches, to which he refuses to apply the positive method, and which he does not study with a critical spirit, but in which he contents himself with the easy and superficial repetition of trite commonplaces.

To those familiar with the former work of the author, this book, from the first page to the last, presents a striking contrast between M. Garofalo, the heterodox criminologist ever ready to criticize with penetration classical criminology, always in revolt against the threadbare commonplaces of juridical tradition, and M. Garofalo, the anti-socialist, the orthodox sociologist, the conservative follower of tradition, who finds that all is well in the world of to-day. He who distinguished himself before by the tone of his publications, always serene and dignified, now permits us to think, that he is less convinced of the correctness of his position than he would have us believe, and to cover up this deficiency of conviction screams and shouts at the top of his voice.

For instance, on page 17, in a style which is neither aristocratic nor bourgeois, he writes that "Bebel had the *impudence* to defend the Commune in a public session of the Reichstag;" and he forgets that the Commune of Paris is not to be judged historically by relying solely upon the revolting impressions left upon the mind by the artificial and exaggerated accounts of the bourgeois press of that time. Malon and Marx have shown by indisputable documentary evidence and on impregnable historical grounds what the verdict on the Commune of the impartial judgment must be, in spite of the excesses which—as M. Alfred Maury said to me at the Père-Lachaise, one day in 1879—were far surpassed by the ferocity of a bloody and savage repression.

In the same way, on pages 20-22, he speaks (I can not see why) of the "contempt" of Marxian socialists for sentimental socialism, which no Marxian has ever dreamt of *despising*, though we recognize it is little in harmony with the systematic, experimental method of social science.

And, on page 154, he seems to think, he is carrying on a scientific discussion when he writes: "In truth, when one sees men who profess such doctrines succeed in obtaining a hearing, one is obliged to recognize that there are no limits to human imbecility."

Ah! my dear Baron Garofalo, how this language reminds me of that of some of the classical criminologists—do you remember it?—who tried to combat the positivist school with language too much like this of yours, which conceals behind hackneyed phrases, the utter lack of ideas to oppose to the hated, but victorious heresy!

But aside from this language, so strange from the pen of M. Garofalo, it is impossible not to perceive the strange contrast between his critical talent and the numerous statements in this book which are, to say the least, characterized by a naiveté one would never have suspected in him.

It is true that, on page 74, like an individualist of the good old days, and with an absolutism which we may henceforth call pre-historic, he deplores the enactment of even those civil laws which have limited the *jus utendi et abutendi* (freely, the right of doing what one will with one's own—Tr.), and which have "seriously maimed the institution of private property," since, he says, "the lower classes suffer cruelly, not from the existence of great fortunes, but rather from the economic embarrassment of the upper classes" (page 77). What boldness of critical thought and profundity in economic science!

And, in regard to my statement that contemporary science is altogether dominated by the idea and the fact of the *social aggregate*—and, therefore, of socialism—in contrast to the glorification of the individual, and, therefore, of individualism, which obtained in the Eighteenth Century, M. Garofalo replies to me that "the story of Robinson Crusoe was borrowed from a very trustworthy history," and adds that it would be possible to cite many cases of anchorites and hermits "who had no need of the company of their fellows" (page 82).

He believes that he has thus demonstrated that I was mistaken when I declared that the species is the sole eternal reality of life and that the individual—himself a biological aggregation—does not live alone and by himself alone, but only by virtue of the fact that he forms a part of a collectivity, to which he owes all the creative conditions of his material, moral and intellectual existence.

In truth, if M. Garofalo had employed such arguments to expose the absurdities of metaphysical penology, and to defend the heresies of the positive school, the latter would certainly not number him among its most eloquent and suggestive founders and champions.

———

And yet, M. Garofalo, instead of repeating these soporific banalities, ought to have been able to discuss seriously the fundamental thesis of socialism, which, through the social ownership of the land and the means of production, tends to assure to every individual the conditions of an existence more worthily human, and of a full and perfectly free development of his physical and moral personality. For then only, when the daily bread of the body and mind is guaranteed, will every man be able, as Goethe said, "to become that which he is," instead of wasting and wearing himself out in the spasmodic and exhausting struggle for daily bread, obtained too often at the expense of personal dignity or the sacrifice of intellectual aptitudes, while human energies are obviously squandered to the great disadvantage of the entire society, and all this with the appearance of personal liberty, but, in fact, with the vast majority of mankind reduced to dependence upon the class in possession of economic monopoly.

But M. Garofalo has altogether refrained from these discussions, which admit of scientific arguments on either hand. He has confined himself, on the contrary, even when he has attempted to discuss seriously, to the repetition of the most superficial commonplaces.

Thus, for example (page 92), opposing the socialists who maintain that the variations of the social environment will inevitably bring about a change in individual aptitudes and activities, he writes: "But the world can not change, if men do not first begin by transforming themselves under the influence of those two ideal factors: honor and duty."

That is the same as saying that a man must not jump into the water ... unless he has learned beforehand to swim, while remaining on land.

Nothing, on the contrary, is more in harmony with the scientific inductions of biology and sociology than the socialist idea, according to which changes in the environment cause correlative changes, both physiological and psychical, in individuals. The soul of Darwinism, is it not wholly in the variability, organic and functional, of individuals and species, under the modifying influence of the environment, fixed and transmitted by natural selection? And neo-Darwinism itself, does it not consist wholly in the constantly increasing importance attributed to the changes in the environment as explanations of the variations of living beings?

And, in the realm of sociology, just as, according to the repeated and unquestioned demonstrations of Spencer, in the passage of human societies from the military type to the industrial type—as Saint-Simon had already pointed out—a change, a process of adaptation, also takes place in that "human nature" which the anti-socialists would have us believe is a fixed and immutable thing, like the "created species" of old-school biology; in the same way, in the gradual transition to a collectivist organization, human nature will necessarily adapt itself to the modified social conditions.

Certainly, human nature will not change in its fundamental tendencies; and, as an illustration, man like the animals will always shun suffering and strive after pleasure, since the former is a diminution and the latter an augmentation of life; but this is not inconsistent with the fact that the application and direction of these biological tendencies can and must change with the changes in the environment. So that I have been able elsewhere to demonstrate that individual egoism will, indeed, always exist, but it will act in a profoundly different fashion, in a society whose conscious goal will be true human solidarity, from the way in which it acts in the individualist and morally anarchical world of to-day, a world in which every man, by the working of what is called "free competition," is forced to follow the impulses of his anti-social egoism, that is to say, to be in conflict, and not in harmony, with the wants and the tendencies of the other members of society.

But the repetition of worn-out commonplaces reaches its climax when M. Garofalo—surely, through inattention—writes these marvelous lines:

"Apparently, many young men of aristocratic families do not work. It is nevertheless more correct to say that they do not do any productive labor for themselves, but they work just the same (!!), and this for the benefit of others!

"In fact, these gentlemen 'of leisure' are generally devoted to sport—hunting, yachting, horseback riding, fencing—or to travel, or to *dilettantisme* in the arts, and their activity, unproductive for themselves, provides an immense number of persons with profitable occupations" (page 183).

One day, when I was studying the prisoners in a jail, one of them said to me: Such an outcry is made against the criminals because they do not work; but if we did not exist, "an immense number of persons"—jailers, policemen, judges and lawyers—would be without a "profitable occupation!"

After having noted these *specimens* of unscientific carelessness, and before entering upon the examination of the few scientific arguments developed by M. Garofalo, it will be well, to aid us in forming a general judgment on his book, to show how far he has forgotten the most elementary rules of the scientific method.

And it will be useful also to add a few examples of mistakes in regard to facts bearing either on science in general, or on the doctrines combated by him.

On page 41, speaking of the scientific work of Marx with a disdain which can not be taken seriously, since it is too much like that of the theologians for Darwin or that of the jurists for Lombroso, he reasons in this curious fashion:

"Starting from the hypothesis that all private property is unjust, it is not logic that is wanting in the doctrine of Marx. But *if one recognizes*, on the contrary, *that every individual has a right to possess some thing of his own*, the direct and inevitable consequence is [the rightfulness of] the profits of capital, and, therefore, the augmentation of the latter."

Certainly, if one admits *a priori* the right of individual property in the land and the means of production ... it is needless and useless to discuss the question.

But the troublesome fact is that all the scientific work of Marx and the socialists has been done precisely in order to furnish absolute scientific proof of the true genesis of capitalist property—the unpaid surplus-labor of the laborer—and to put an end to the old fables about "the first occupant," and "accumulated savings" which are only exceptions, ever becoming rarer.

- 118 -

Moreover, the negation of private property is not "the hypothesis," but the logical and inevitable consequence of the premises of *facts* and of *historical* demonstrations made, not only by Marx, but by a numerous group of sociologists who, abandoning the reticence and mental reservations of orthodox conventionalism, have, by that step, become socialists.

But contemporary socialism, for the very reason that it is in perfect harmony with scientific and exact thought, no longer harbors the illusions of those who fancy that to-morrow—with a dictator of "wonderful intelligence and remarkable eloquence," charged with the duty of organizing collectivism by means of decrees and regulations—we could reach the Co-operative Commonwealth at a bound, eliminating the intermediate phases. Moreover, is not the absolute and unbridled individualism of yesterday already transformed into a limited individualism and into a partial collectivism by legal limitations of the *jus abutendi* and by the continuous transformation into social functions or public properties of the services (lighting, water-supply, transportation, etc.), or properties (roads, bridges, canals, etc.), which were formerly private services and properties? These intermediate phases can not be suppressed by decrees, but they develop and finish their course naturally day by day, under the pressure of the economic and social conditions; but, by a natural and therefore inexorable progress, they are constantly approaching more closely that ultimate phase of absolute collectivism in the means of production, which the socialists have not invented, but the tendency toward which they have shown, and whose ultimate attainment they scientifically predict. The rate of progress toward this goal they can accelerate by giving to the proletarians, organized into a class-party, a clearer consciousness of their historic mission.

All through this book are scattered not only defects of method, but also actual errors in matters of fact. The book is also marred by an immanent contradiction that runs all through it, in connection with the absolutely uncompromising attitude against socialism which the author aims to maintain, but which he is unable to keep up in the face of the irresistible tendency of the facts, as we shall see in the conclusion of this analysis.

In chapter IV, M. Garofalo contends that civilization would be menaced with destruction by the elevation to power of the popular classes. M. Garofalo, who is of an old aristocratic family, declares that "the Third Estate, which should have substituted youthful energies for the feebleness and corruption of an effete and degenerate aristocracy, has shown magnified *a hundred-fold* the defects and corruption of the latter" (p. 206). This is certainly not a correct historical judgment; for it is certain that the Third Estate, which with the French Revolution gained political ascendancy—a political ascendancy made inevitable by its previously won economic ascendancy,—gave in the course of the Nineteenth Century a new and powerful impulse to civilization. And if to-day, after a century of undisputed domination, the bourgeoisie shows "multiplied a hundred-fold" the defects and the corruption of the aristocracy of the Eighteenth Century, this signifies simply that the Third Estate has reached the final phase of its parabola, so that the advent of a more developed social phase is becoming an imminent historical necessity.

Another error in criminal psychology—natural enough for idealists and metaphysicians, but which may well surprise us in an exact scientist—is the influence upon human conduct which M. Garofalo attributes to the religious sentiment. "Moral instruction has no meaning, or at least no efficacy, without a religious basis" (p. 267). And from this erroneous psychological premise, he draws the conclusion that it is necessary to return to religious instruction in the schools, "selecting the masters from among men of mature age, fathers of families or *ministers of religion*" (p. 268).

In combating this conclusion, truly surprising in a scientist, it is useless to recall the teachings of the experience of former times in regard to the pretended moralizing influence of the priest upon the school; and it is also unnecessary to recall the statistics of criminal assaults committed by priests condemned to celibacy. It is equally superfluous to add that at all events, in again turning the priest into a schoolmaster, it would be necessary to recommend to him never to recall the invectives of Jesus against the rich, the metaphor of the camel passing through the eye of a needle, or the still more violent invectives of the Fathers of the Church against private property; for long before Proudhon, Saint Jerome had said that "wealth is always the product of theft; if it was not committed by the present holder, it was by his ancestors," and Saint Ambrose added that "Nature has established community [of goods]; from usurpation alone is private property born."

If it is true that later on the Church, in proportion as it departed from the doctrines of the Master, preached in favor of the rich, leaving to the poor the hope of Paradise; and if it is true, as M. Garofalo says, that "the Christian philosophers exhorted the poor to sanctify the tribulations of poverty by resignation" (p. 166); it is also true that, for example, Bossuet, in one of his famous sermons, recognized that "the complaints of the poor are justified;" and he asked: "Why are conditions so unequal? We are all formed of the same dust, and nothing can justify it." So that recently, M. Giraud-Teulon, in the name of an hermaphrodite liberalism, recalled that "the right of private property is rather tolerated by the Church as an existing fact than presented as a necessary foundation of civil society. It is even condemned in its inspiring principle by the Fathers of the Church."[91]

But apart from all this, it is sufficient for me to establish that the psychological premise, from which M. Garofalo starts, is erroneous in itself.

Studying elsewhere the influence of the religious sentiment on criminality[92], I have shown by positive documentary evidence, that religious beliefs, efficacious for individuals already endowed with a normal social sense, since they add to the sanction of the moral conscience (which, however, would suffice by itself) the sanctions of the life beyond the tomb—"religion is the guarantor of justice"[93]—are, nevertheless, wholly ineffective, when the social sense, on account of some physio-psychical anomaly, is atrophied or non-existent. So that religious belief, considered as a regulator of social conduct, is at once superfluous for honorable people and altogether ineffective for those who are not honorable, if indeed it is not capable of increasing the propensity to evil by developing religious fanaticism or giving rise to the hope of pardon in the confessional or of absolution *in articulo mortis*, etc.

It is possible to understand—at least as an expedient as utilitarian as it is highly hypocritical—the argument of those who, atheists so far as they themselves are concerned, still wish to preserve religious beliefs for the people, because they exercise a depressing influence and prevent all energetic agitation for human rights and enjoyments *here below*. The conception of God as a Policeman is only one among many illusions.

———

Besides these errors of fact in the biological and psychological sciences, M. Garofalo also misstates the socialist doctrines, following the example of the opponents of the new school of criminology, who found it easier to refute the doctrines they attributed to us than to shake the doctrines we defended.

On page 14, M. Garofalo begins by stating, "the true tendency of the party known as the Workingmen's Party, is to gain power, *not in the interest of all,* but in order to expropriate the dominant class and *to step into their shoes.* They do not disguise this purpose in their programmes." This statement is found again on page 210, etc.

Now, it suffices to have read the programme of the socialist party, from the MANIFESTO of Marx and Engels down to the propagandist publications, to know, on the contrary, that contemporary socialism wishes, and declares its wish, to accomplish the general suppression of all social divisions into classes by suppressing the division of the social patrimony of production, and, therefore, proclaims itself resolved to achieve the prosperity OF ALL, and not only—as some victims of myopia continue to believe—that of a Fourth Estate, which would simply have to follow the example of the decaying Third Estate.

Starting from this fundamental datum of socialism, that *every individual*, unless he be a child, sick or an invalid, *must work, in order to live*, at one sort or another of useful labor, it follows as an inevitable consequence that, in a society organized on this principle, all class antagonism will become impossible; for this antagonism exists only when society contains a great majority who work, in order to live in discomfort, and a small minority who live well, without working.

This initial error naturally dominates the entire book. Thus, for instance, the third chapter is devoted to proving that "the social revolution planned for by the new socialists, will be the destruction of all *moral order* in society, because it is without an *ideal* to serve it as a luminous standard" (p. 159).

Let us disregard, my dear Baron, the famous "moral order" of that society which enriches and honors the well-dressed wholesale thieves of the great and little Panamas, the banks and railways, and condemns to imprisonment children and women who steal dry wood or grass in the fields which formerly belonged to the commune.

But to say that socialism is without an *ideal*, when even its opponents concede to it this immense superiority in potential strength over the sordid skepticism of the present world, *viz.*, its ardent faith in a higher social justice for all, a faith that makes strikingly clear its resemblance to the regenerating Christianity of primitive times (very different from that "fatty degeneration" of Christianity, called Catholicism), to say this is truly, for a scientist, to blindly rebel against the most obvious facts of daily life.

M. Garofalo even goes so far as to say that "the want of the necessaries of life" is a very exceptional fact, and that therefore the condition of "the proletariat is a *social condition* like that of all the other classes, and the lack of capital, which is its characteristic, is a permanent economic condition *which is not at all abnormal* FOR THOSE WHO ARE USED TO IT."[94]

Then—while passing over this comfortable and egoistic quietism which finds nothing abnormal in the misery ... of others—we perceive how deficient M. Garofalo is, in the most elementary accuracy, in the ascertainment of facts when we recall the suffering and ever-growing multitude of the *unemployed*, which is sometimes a "local and transitory" phenomenon, but which, in its acute or chronic forms, is always the necessary and incontestable effect of capitalist accumulation and the introduction and improvement of machinery, which are, in their turn, the source of modern socialism, scientific socialism, so different from the sentimental socialism of former times.

But the fundamental fallacy, from which so many thinkers—M. Garofalo among them—can not free themselves, and to which I myself yielded, before I had penetrated, thanks to the Marxian theory of historic materialism—or, more exactly, of economic determinism—into the true spirit of socialist sociology, is the tendency to judge the inductions of socialism by the biological, psychological and sociological data of the present society, without thinking of the necessary changes that will be effected by a different economic environment with its inevitable concomitants or consequences, different moral and political environments.

In M. Garofalo's book we find once more this *petitio principii* which refuses to believe in the future in the name of the present, which is declared immutable. It is exactly as if in the earliest geological epochs it had been concluded from the flora and fauna then existing that it was impossible for a fauna and flora ever to exist differing from them as widely as do the cryptogams from the conifers, or the mammalia from the mollusca.

This confirms, once more, the observation that I made before, that to deny the truth of scientific socialism is implicitly to deny that law of universal and eternal evolution, which is the dominant factor in all modern scientific thought.

On page 16, M. Garofalo predicts that with the triumph of socialism "we shall see re-appear upon earth the reign of irrational and brutal physical force, and that we shall witness, *as happens every day* in the lowest strata of the population, the triumph of the most violent men." And he repeats this on pages 209-210; but he forgets that, given the socialist premise of a better organized social environment, this brutality, which is the product of the present misery and lack of education, must necessarily gradually diminish, and at last disappear.

Now, the possibility of this improvement of the social environment, which socialism asserts, is a thesis that can be discussed; but when a writer, in order to deny this possibility, opposes to the future the effects of a present, whose elimination is the precise question at issue, he falls into that insidious fallacy which it is only necessary to point out to remove all foundation from his arguments.

And it is as always by grace of this same fallacy that he is able to declare, on page 213, that under the socialist regime "the fine arts will be unable to exist. It is easy to say, they will henceforth be exercised and cultivated for the benefit of the public. Of what public? Of the great mass of the people *deprived of artistic education*?" As if, when poverty is once eliminated and labor has become less exhausting for the popular classes, the comfort and economic security, which would result from this, would not be sure to develop in them also the taste for æsthetic pleasure, which they feel and satisfy now, so far as that is possible for them, in the various forms of popular art, or as may be seen to-day it Paris and Vienna by the "*Théâtre socialiste*" and at Brussells by the free musical matinées, instituted by the socialists and frequented by a constantly growing number of workingmen. It is just the same with regard to scientific instruction, as witness "University Extension" in England and Belgium. And all this, notwithstanding the present total lack of artistic education, but thanks to the exigence among the workers of these countries of an economic condition lees wretched than that of the agricultural or even the industrial proletariat in countries such as Italy.

And from another point of view, what are the museums if not a form of collective ownership and use of the products of art?

It is again, as always, the same fallacy which (at page 216) makes M. Garofalo write: "The history of Europe, from the fifth to the thirteenth centuries, shows us, *by analogy*, what would happen to the world if the lower classes should come into power.... How to explain the medieval barbarism and anarchy save by the grossness and ignorance of the conquerors? *The same fate* would inevitably await the modern civilization, if the controlling power should fall into the hands of the proletarians, who, assuredly, *are intellectually not superior to the ancient barbarians* and MORALLY ARE FAR INFERIOR TO THEM!"

Let us disregard this unjustified and unjustifiable insult and this completely erroneous historical comparison. It is enough to point out that it is here supposed that by a stroke of a magic wand "the lower classes" will be able in a single day to gain possession of power without having been prepared for this by a preliminary moral revolution, a revolution accomplished in them by the acquired consciousness of their rights and of their organic solidarity. It will be impossible to compare the proletarians in whom this moral revolution shall have taken place with the barbarians of the Middle Ages.

In my book *Socialismo et Criminalità*, published in 1883, and which to-day my adversaries, including M. Garofalo (p. 128 *et seq.*), try to oppose to the opinions which I have upheld in my more recent book, *Socialisme et science positive* (the present work), I have developed two theses:

I. That the social organization could not be *suddenly* changed, as was then maintained in Italy by the sentimental socialists, since the law of evolution dominates with sovereign power the human world as well as the inorganic and organic world;

II. That, by analogy, crime could not disappear *absolutely* from among mankind, as the Italian socialists of those days vaguely hinted.

Now, in the first place it would not have been at all inconsistent if, after having partially accepted socialism, which I had already done in 1883, the progressive evolution of my thought, after having studied the systematic, scientific form given to socialism by Marx and his co-workers, had led me to recognize (apart from all personal advantage) the complete truth of socialism. But, especially, precisely because scientific socialism (since [the work of] Marx, Engels, Malon, de Paepe, Dramard, Lanessan, Guesde, Schaeffle, George, Bebel, Loria, Colajanni, Turati, de Greef, Lafargue, Jaurès, Renard, Denis, Plechanow, Vandervelde, Letourneau, L. Jacoby, Labriola, Kautsky, etc.) is different from the sentimental socialism which I had alone in mind in 1883, it is for that very reason that I still maintain to-day these two same principal theses, and I find myself in so doing in perfect harmony with international scientific socialism.

And as to the absolute disappearance of all criminality, I still maintain my thesis of 1883, and in the present book (§ 3), I have written that, even under the socialist regime, there will be—though infinitely fewer—some who will be conquered in the struggle for existence and that, though the chronic and epidemic forms of nervous disease, crime, insanity and suicide, are destined to disappear, the acute and sporadic forms will not completely disappear.

At this statement M. Garofalo manifests a surprise which, as I can not suppose it simulated, I declare truly inexplicable in a sociologist and a criminologist; for this reminds me too strongly of the ignorant surprise shown by a review of classical jurisprudence in regard to a new scientific fact recorded by the *Archives de psychiatrie* of M. Lombroso, the case being the disappearance of every criminal tendency in a woman after the surgical removal of her ovaries.

But that the trepanning of the skull in a case of traumatic epilepsy or that ovariotomy can cure the central nervous system and, therefore, restore the character and even the morality of the individual, these are facts that can be unknown only to a metaphysical idealist, an opponent of the positivist school of criminology.

And yet this is how M. Garofalo comments on my induction (p. 240); this commentary is reproduced again on pages 95, 100, 134 and 291:

"It is truly extraordinary that M. Ferri, notwithstanding that criminal anthropology, of which he has so long been (and still is) one of the most ardent partisans, should have allowed himself to be so blinded by the mirage of socialism. A statement such as that which I have quoted at first leaves the reader stunned, since he sees absolutely *no connection* between nervous diseases and collective ownership. It would be just as sensible to say that by the study of algebra one can make sure of one's first-born child being a male." How exactly like the remarks of the Review of jurisprudence concerning the case of the removal of the ovaries!

Now, let us see whether it is possible, by a supreme effort of our feeble intellect, to point out a connection between nervous diseases and collective ownership.

That poverty, *i. e.*, inadequate physical and mental nutrition—in the life of the individual and through hereditary transmission—is, if not the only and exclusive cause, certainly the principal cause of human degeneration, is henceforth an indisputable and undisputed fact.

That the poverty and misery of the working class—and notably of the unhappy triad of the unemployed, the displaced [by machinery, trusts, etc.] and those who have been expropriated by taxation—is destined to disappear with the socialization of the land and the means of production:— this is the proposition that socialism maintains and demonstrates.

It is, therefore, natural that under the socialist régime, with the disappearance of poverty, there should be eliminated the principal source of popular degeneracy in the epidemic and chronic forms of diseases, crimes, insanity and suicide; this can, moreover, be seen at present—on a small scale, but clearly enough to positively confirm the general induction—since diseases [nervous], crimes, insanity and suicide increase during famines and crises, while they diminish in years when the economic conditions are less wretched.

There is still more to be said. Even among the aristocracy and bourgeoisie, no one can fail to see that the feverish competition and cannibalistic strife of our present system beget nervous disorders, crime and suicide, which would be rendered quite unnecessary by the establishment of a socialist régime, which would banish worry and uneasiness for the morrow from the human race.

There then you see established the relation between collective ownership and nervous diseases or degeneration in general, not only among the popular and more numerous classes, but also in the bourgeois and aristocratic classes.

It is, indeed, astonishing that the anti-socialist prejudice of M. Garofalo should have been strong enough to cause him to forget that truth which is nevertheless a legitimate induction of criminal biology and sociology, the truth that besides the congenital criminal there are other types of criminals who are more numerous and more directly produced by the vitiated social environment. And, finally, if the congenital criminal is not himself the direct product of the environment, he is indirectly its product through the degeneration begun in his ancestors, by some acute disease in some cases, but by debilitating poverty in the majority of cases, and afterward hereditarily transmitted and aggravated in accordance with the inexorable laws discovered by modern science.

M. Garofalo's book, which was announced as an assault of science upon socialism, has been, even from this point of view, a complete disappointment, as even the Italian anti-socialists have confessed in several of the most orthodox Reviews.

It now remains for me to reply briefly to his observations—and they are few and far between—on the relations which exist between contemporary socialism and the general trend and tendency of thought in the exact sciences.

Disregarding the arguments which I had developed on this subject by pointing out that there is an essential connection between economic and social transmutation (Marx) and the theories of biological transmutation (Darwin) and of universal transmutation (Spencer), M. Garofalo has thought it prudent to take up for consideration only "the struggle for existence" and the relations between "evolution and revolution."

As to the first, five pages (96-100) are enough to enable him to declare, without supporting his declaration by any positive argument which is not merely a different verbal expression of the same idea, that the Darwinian law of the struggle for existence has not undergone and can not undergo any transformation except that which will change the violent struggle into competition (the struggle of skill and intelligence) and that this law is irreconcilable with socialism; for it necessarily requires the sacrifice of the conquered, while socialism "would guarantee to all men their material existence, so they would have no cause for anxiety."

But my friend, the Baron Garofalo, quietly and completely ignores the fundamental argument that the socialists oppose to the individualist interpretation that has hitherto been given of the struggle for life and which still affects the minds of some socialists so far as to make them think that the law of the struggle for life is not true and that Darwinism is irreconcilable with socialism.

The socialists, in fact, think that the laws of life are the following, and that they are concurrent and inseparable: *the struggle for existence* and *solidarity in the struggle against natural forces*. If the first law is in spirit individualist, the second is essentially socialistic.

Now, not to repeat what I have written elsewhere, it is sufficient here for me to establish this positive fact that all human evolution is effected through the constantly increasing predominance of the law of solidarity over the law of the struggle for existence.

The forms of the struggle are transformed and grow milder, as I showed as long ago as 1883, and M. Garofalo accepts this way of looking at the matter when he recognizes that the muscular struggle is ever tending to become an intellectual struggle. But he has in view only the formal evolution; he wholly disregards the progressive decrease in the importance of the struggling function under the action of the other parallel law of solidarity in the struggle.

Here comes in that constant principle in sociology, that the social forms and forces co-exist always, but that their relative importance changes from epoch to epoch and from place to place.

Just as in the individual egoism and altruism co-exist and will co-exist always—for egoism is the basis of personal existence—but with a continuous and progressive restriction and transformation of egoism, corresponding to the expansion of altruism, in passing from the fierce egoism of savage humanity to the less brutal egoism of the present epoch, and finally to the more fraternal egoism of the coming society; in the same way in the social organism, for example, the military type and the industrial type always co-exist, but with a progressively increasing predominance of the latter over the former.

The same truth applies to the different forms of the family, and also to many other institutions, of which Spencerian sociology had given only the *descriptive* evolution and of which the Marxian theory of economic determinism has given the *genetic* evolution, by explaining that the religious and juridical customs and institutions, the social types, the forms of the family, etc., are only the reflex of the economic structure which differs in varying localities (on islands or continents, according to the abundance or scarcity of food) and also varies from epoch to epoch. And—to complete the Marxian theory—this economic structure is, in the case of each social group, the resultant of its race energies developing themselves in such or such a physical environment, at I have said elsewhere.

The same rule holds in the case of the two co-existing laws of the *struggle for existence* and of *solidarity in the struggle*, the first of which predominates where the economic conditions are more difficult; while the second predominates with the growth of the economic security of the majority. But while this security will become complete under the régime of socialism, which will assure to every man who works the material means of life, this will not exclude the intellectual forms of the struggle for existence which M. Tchisch recently said should be interpreted not only in the sense of a *struggle for life*, but also in the sense of a *struggle for the enrichment of life*.[95]

In fact, when once the material life of every one is assured, together with the duty of labor for *all* the members of society, man will continue always to struggle *for the enrichment of life*, that is to say, for the fuller development of his physical and moral individuality. And it is only under the régime of socialism that, the predominance of the law of solidarity being decisive, the struggle for existence will change its form and substance, while persisting as an eternal striving toward a better life in the *solidaire* development of the individual and the collectivity.

But M. Garofalo devotes more attention to the practical (?) relations between socialism and the law of evolution. And in *substance*, once more making use of the objection already so often raised against Marxism and its tactics, he formulates his indictment thus:

"The new socialists who, on the one hand, pretend to speak in the name of sociological science and of the natural laws of evolution, declare themselves politically, on the other hand, as revolutionists. Now, evidently science has nothing to do with their political action. Although they take pains to say that by "revolution" they do not mean either a riot or a revolt—an explanation also contained in the dictionary[96]—this fact always remains, *viz.*: that they are unwilling to await the *spontaneous* organization of society under the new economic arrangement foreseen by them in a more or less remote future. For if they should thus quietly await its coming, who among them would survive to prove to the incredulous the truth of their predictions?

It is a question then of an evolution *artificially hastened*, that is to say, in other words, of the *use of force* to transform society in accordance with their wishes." (p. 30.)

"The socialists of the Marxian school do not expect the transformation to be effected by a slow evolution, but by a *revolution of the people*, and they even fix the epoch of its occurence." (p. 53.)

"Henceforth the socialists must make a decision and take one horn of the dilemma or the other.

"Either they must be *theoretical evolutionists*, WHO WAIT PATIENTLY until the time shall be ripe;

Or, on the contrary, they must be *revolutionary democrats*; and if they take this horn, it is nonsense to talk of evolution, accumulation, spontaneous concentration, etc. ACCOMPLISH THEN THIS REVOLUTION, IF YOU HAVE THE POWER." (p. 151.)

I do not wish to dwell on this curious "instigation to civil war" by such an orthodox conservative as the Baron Garofalo, although he might be suspected of the not specially Christian wish to see this "revolution of the people" break out at once, while the people are still disorganized and weak and while it would be easier for the dominant class to bleed them copiously....

Let us try rather to deliver M. Garofalo from another trouble; for on page 119 he exclaims pathetically: "I declare on my honor I do not understand how a sincere socialist can to-day be a revolutionist. I would be sincerely grateful to anyone who would explain this to me, for to me this is an enigma, so great is the contradiction between the theory and the methods of the socialists."

Well then, console yourself, my excellent friend! Just as in the case of the relationship between collective ownership and human degeneration, which seemed so "enigmatical" to this same Baron Garofalo—and although he has not offered his gratitude for the solution of this enigma to the socialist Oedipus who explained it to him—here also, in the case of this other enigma, the explanation is very simple.

On the subject of the social question the attitudes assumed in the domain of science, or on the field of politics, are the following:

1st. That of the *conservatives*, such as M. Garofalo. These, judging the world, not by the conditions objectively established, but by their own subjective impressions, consider that they are well enough off under the present régime, and contend that everything is for the best in this best of all possible worlds, and oppose in all cases, with a very logical egoism, every change which is not merely a superficial change;

2nd. That of the *reformers*, who, like all the eclectics, whose number is infinite, give, as the Italian proverb says, one blow to the cask and another to the hoop and do not deny—O, no!—the inconveniences and even the absurdities of the present ... but, not to compromise themselves too far, hasten to say that they must confine themselves to minor ameliorations, to superficial reforms, that is to say, to treating the symptoms instead of the disease, a therapeutic method as easy and as barren of abiding results in dealing with the social organism as with the individual organism;

3rd. That, finally, of the *revolutionaries*, who rightly call themselves thus because they think and say that the effective remedy is not to be found in superficial reforms, but in a radical reorganization of society, beginning at the very foundation, private property, and which will be so profound that it will truly constitute a social revolution.

It is in this sense that Galileo accomplished a scientific revolution; for he did not confine himself to reforms of the astronomical system received in his time, but he radically changed its fundamental lines. And it is in this same sense that Jacquart effected an industrial revolution, since he did not confine himself to reforming the hand-loom, as it had existed for centuries, but radically changed its structure and productive power.

Therefore, when socialists speak of socialism as *revolutionary*, they mean by this to describe the programme to be realized and the final goal to be attained and not—as M. Garofalo, in spite of the dictionary, continues to believe—the method or the tactics to be employed in achieving this goal, the social revolution.

And right here appears the profound difference between the method of sentimental socialism and that of scientific socialism—henceforth the only socialism in the civilized world—which has received through the work of Marx, Engels and their successors that systematic form which is the distinctive mark of all the *evolutionary* sciences. And that is why and how I have been able to demonstrate that contemporary socialism is in full harmony with the scientific doctrine of evolution.

Socialism is in fact evolutionary, but not in the sense that M. Garofalo prefers of "waiting patiently until the times shall be ripe" and until society "shall organize *spontaneously* under the new economic arrangement," as if science necessarily must consist in Oriental contemplation and academic Platonism—as it has done for too long—instead of investigating the conditions of actual, every-day life, and applying its inductions to them.

Certainly, "science for the sake of science," is a formula very satisfactory to the avowed conservatives—and that is only logical—and also to the eclectics; but modern positivism prefers the formula of "science for life's sake" and, therefore, thinks that "the ripeness of the times" and "the new economic arrangement" will certainly not be realized by spontaneous generation and that therefore it is necessary to act, in harmony with the inductions of science, in order to bring this realization to pass.

To act, but *how*?

There is the question of methods and tactics, which differentiates utopian socialism from scientific socialism; the former fancied it possible to alter the economic organization of society from top to bottom by the improvised miracle of a popular insurrection; the latter, on the contrary, declares that the law of evolution is supreme and that, therefore, the social revolution can be nothing but the final phase of a preliminary evolution, which will consist—through scientific study and propaganda work—in the realization of the exhortation of Marx: *Proletarians of all countries, unite!*

There then is the explanation of the *easy* enigma, presented by the fact that socialism, though revolutionary in its programme, follows the laws of evolution in its method of realization, and that is the secret of its vitality and power, and that is also what makes it so essentially different from that mystical and violent anarchism, which class prejudices or the exigencies of venal journalism assert is nothing but a consequence of socialism, while in fact it is the practical negation of socialism.

―――――

Finally, as a synthetic conclusion, I think it worth while to show that, while in the beginning of his book M. Garofalo starts out in open hostility to socialism with the intention of maintaining an absolutely uncompromising attitude, declaring on the first page that he has written his book "for those who are called the bourgeois," in order to dissuade them from the concessions which they themselves, in their own minds, can not prevent themselves from making to the undeniable truth of the socialist ideal, when he reaches the end of his polemic, the irresistible implications of the facts force M. Garofalo to a series of eclectic compromises, which produce on the reader, after so many accusations and threats of repression, the depressing impression of a mental collapse, as unforeseen as it is significant.

Indeed, M. Garofalo, on page 258, recognizes the usefulness of combinations of laborers to enable them "to *resist* unjust demands," and even declares it obligatory upon factory-owners "to assure a life-pension to their laborers who have served them long." (p. 275.) And he demands for the laborers at all events "a share in the profits" (p. 276); he recognizes also that the adult out of work and in good health has the right to assistance, no less than the sick man or the cripple (p. 281).

M. Garofalo, who by all these restrictions to his absolute individualism has permitted himself to make concessions to Socialism, which are in flagrant contradiction with his announced intention and to the whole trend of his book, ends indeed by confessing that "if the new socialists were to preach collectivism *solely within the sphere of agricultural industry*, it would at least be possible to discuss it, since one would not be confronted at the outset by an absurdity, as is the case in attempting to discuss universal collectivism. This is not equivalent to saying that agricultural collectivism[97] would be *easily* put into practice."

That is to say that there is room for compromises and that a mitigated collectivism would not be in contradiction with all the laws of science, a contradiction which it seems his entire argument was intended to establish; for M. Garofalo confines himself to remarking that the realization of collectivism in land would not be *easy*—a fact that no socialist has ever disputed.

There is no need for me to point out once more how this method of combating socialism, on the part of M. Garofalo, resemble that which the classical criminologists employed against the positivist school, when, after so many sweeping denials of our teachings, they came to admit that, nevertheless, some of our inductions, for example, the anthropological classification of criminals, might well be applied ... on a reduced scale, in the administration of jails and penitentiaries, but never in the provisions of the criminal law!

During many years, as a defender of the positivist school of criminology, I have had personal experience of the inevitable phases that must be passed through by a scientific truth before its final triumph—the conspiracy of silence; the attempt to smother the new idea with ridicule; then, in consequence of the resistance to these artifices of reactionary conservatism, the new ideas are misrepresented, through ignorance or to facilitate assaults upon them, and at last they are partially admitted and that is the beginning of the final triumph.

So that, knowing these phases of the natural evolution of every new idea, now when, for the second time, instead of resting upon the laurels of my first scientific victories, I have wished to fight for a second and more radical heresy; this time the victory appears to me more certain, since my opponents and my former companions in arms again call into use against it the same artifices of reactionary opposition, whose impotence I had already established on a narrower battle-field, but one where the conflict was neither less keen nor less difficult.

And so, a new recruit enlisted to fight for a grand and noble human ideal, I behold even now the spectacle of partial and inevitable concessions being wrung from those who still pretend to maintain a position of uncompromising and unbending hostility, but who are helpless before the great cry of suffering and hope which springs from the depths of the masses of mankind in passionate emotion and in intellectual striving.

ENRICO FERRI.

FOOTNOTES:

[89] This appendix was written as a reply to a book by Baron Garofalo, called *La Superstition socialiste*. This book made quite a sensation in Italy and France, not on account of the solidity of its arguments, but merely because Garofalo had been associated with Lombroso and Ferri in founding the modern school of criminology. As Garofalo's book is practically unknown in this country, I have felt justified in making many and large omissions from this appendix. Gabriel Deville exposed the emptiness of Garofalo's pretentious book in a most brilliant open letter to the Baron, which appeared in *Le Socialiste* for the 15th of Sept., 1895.—Tr.

[90] The present work, which appeared in Italian in 1894, in French in 1895, and in Spanish in Madrid and Buenos-Ayres in 1895. It now appears in English for the first time.

[91] GIRAUD-TEULON, *Double péril social. L'Eglise et le socialisme*, Paris, 1894, p. 17.

[92] E. FERRI, *l'Omicidio nell' antropologia criminale*, Turin, 1895, together with *Atlas* and more especially *Religion et Criminalité* in *la Revue des Revues*, Oct.. 1895.

[93] DE MOLINARI, *Science et Religion*, Paris, 1894.

[94] Garofalo suppressed these lines in the French edition of his book.

[95] Tchisch, *la Loi fondamentale de la vie*, Dorpat, 1895, p. 19.

[96] And yet, how many judges have not, to the injury of the Socialists, denied this elementary truth taught by the dictionary!

[97] More correctly, collective ownership of the land.—Tr.